Nuneaton, Coventry & Leamington Railway

— PETER LEE —

This edition first published 2013.

Amberley Publishing
The Hill, Stroud
Gloucestershire, GL5 4EP

www.amberleybooks.com

British Library Cataloguing in Publication Data.
A catalogue record for this book is available from the British Library.

ISBN 978-1-4456-0661-3

Typesetting and Origination by Amberley Publishing.
Printed in the UK.

Contents

Introduction

The railways that connected Nuneaton to Coventry and Coventry to Leamington Spa were among the earliest branch lines built for the London & North Western Railway. For many years they were operated as one continuous railway with through passenger services providing a link from the West Coast Main Line to the former Great Western Main Line. It was a useful cross-country route providing good connections and handy diversions for the travelling public. Both sections of line had a very different character. The Nuneaton to Coventry section penetrated rich coalfields, particularly the Nuneaton and Longford section; the Longford to Coventry section ran through the engineering works and car plants for which that city was famous; the Leamington branch was rural in aspect, although it did have several brickyards and local businesses on its route.

Both lines prospered in their heyday and were extremely busy with all manner of freight as well as intensive and highly utilised passenger traffic, particularly for workers in the Coventry engineering plants, which generated a huge volume of journeys in the peak hours. Then, in the 1960s, British Railways accountants decided they were no longer viable, although even then passenger traffic was still very brisk. In addition, many of the industries serviced by the line closed down or went over to road transport. The lines closed to passenger traffic, although both sections were reopened a few years later. Freight traffic never entirely disappeared. Today, through freight traffic on this route is heavier than ever, as Freightliner trains between Southampton, Birmingham and the North traverse its entire course regularly. There is a little sporadic freight to Prologis Park on the outskirts of Coventry and deliveries of fuel to the Murco sidings in Bedworth. Modern developments have encouraged a renaissance of the line, which will reach fruition in the next few years as new stations are opened and through passenger services reintroduced. This book documents the old lines in the days of steam and early diesels.

It is not possible with the passage of time to give you a day-by-day account of the history of the two lines under review. I can only provide a window or snapshot. Hopefully, if your interest goes beyond this book, it will provide a modest amount of context. There is little coverage of modern diesel haulage, as that is for the modern enthusiast in the future.

Abbreviations Used in the Text

British Railways (1948 onwards), on nationalisation (BR)
Inside Cylinder (IC)
London & Birmingham Railway (L&B)

London Midland & Scottish Railway (successor to the LNWR & MR on grouping in 1923) (1923–48) (LMS)
London & North Western Railway (1846–1923) (LNWR)
Midland Railway (1842–1923) (MR)
National Coal Board (1947 onwards) (NCB)
Outside Cylinder (OC)

Acknowledgements

As usual, I must thank a wide variety of good old friends and correspondents who have shared their memories and archive material with me. I hope this helps put together a story of a journey back in time in the 'good old days' of a line that is about to be transformed into a modern cross-country railway serving new customers with a new historical future.

Maurice Billington, Gordon Webster, Ray Fox, Michael J. Lee, Mike Kinder, Dennis Labram, Roy Heatherington, Geoff & Madge Edmands, Gordon Webster, David Stubbs, Ted Prince, Ted Talbot, Andy Lowe, Peter Bayly, Anne Gore, Ernie Haywood, Ray Smith, H. C. Casserley, Mike Mensing, Andy & Mary Lowe, Mike Musson, Reg Kimber, Keith Draper, Mike Christensen, G. H. Coltas, Vic and Bill Holloway, A. G. Ellis, J. A. Peden, George and Roger Carpenter Alliez, David Fordham, Peter Ellis, Alan Cook, John Burton, Harry Addison, Keith Lambourne, Edgar Barnsby, Eric Tonks, Laurence Fretwell, Ray Shill, the Industrial Railway Society, Nuneaton Library, *The Nuneaton News*, *Coventry Evening Telegraph*, the Railway Correspondence & Travel Society, the London & North Western Railway Society, the Stephenson Locomotive Society. Enhanced Nuneaton shed allocation information was prepared by Alan Cook, with Ray Fox and Mike Kinder's amendments.

BIBLIOGRAPHY

Biddle, Gordon, 'The Railway Monopoly at Coventry'. An article in the *Railway World* (February 1962)
Christensen, Mike, *Coventry Station* (British Railways Journal No. 51, Spring 1994)
Clinker, C. R., *Railways of the West Midlands 1808–1954* (Stephenson Locomotive Society)
Longworth, Hugh, *British Railways Steam Allocations* (Ian Allan Publications)
Yeadon, W. B., *A Compendium of LNWR Locomotives 1912–64* (Vols 1 & 2)

The Opening

The Coventry to Nuneaton line was conceived as a branch of the London & Birmingham Railway before that company became a major part of the London & North Western Railway in 1846. Mr Francis Stevenson (1827–1902) was engaged as the engineer to the London & Birmingham Railway, and he also become the resident engineer for the Coventry & Nuneaton line. The L&B had recognised the mineral wealth along the route and the line was sited to take maximum advantage of this.

The branch was laid out along coal outcrops for 5 miles at the Nuneaton/Bedworth end, where there were numerous collieries and brickyards. Part of the original Act called for branches to be laid into Griff, Mount Pleasant and Victoria Collieries. These connections were soon expanded, with a vast array of tracks and connections leading off into every conceivable industrial outlet along the line.

ACTS OF PARLIAMENT

Coventry, Nuneaton, Birmingham & Leicester, 27 July 1846
Acts 9 & 10 Victoria, Chapter 253, incorporation of company and construction powers sought from Nuneaton junction with the Trent Valley Railway to Wigston Junction and, on 22 July 1847, Act 10 & 11 Victoria, Chapter 270, power to sell to the LNWR and/or the Midland Railway and transfer powers under the 1846 Act. This line was not built.

3 August 1846
Acts 9 & 10 Victoria, Chapter 331, construction powers were sought for a line between Coventry and Nuneaton on the current alignment and a direct spur to be built through to the Coventry, Nuneaton, Birmingham and Leicester line. This spur was not built.

2 July 1847
Acts 10 & 11 Victoria, Chapter 110, the Oxford, Coventry & Burton on Trent line was proposed and capital was sought for a line from Coventry to Nuneaton.

14 August 1848
Additional Powers Act 11 & 12 Victoria, Chapter 130, construction powers sought to Craven Colliery and Bedworth to Mount Pleasant and to Victoria Colliery.

20 September 1847
The Parliamentary estimate for the line was £232,026.

18 June 1857
The tender of Thomas Hayton of Kilsby was accepted at £144,025 16s 11d

(Coventry & Nuneaton Minutes Books PRO Kew)

Nuneaton Trent Valley Station

Above: Nuneaton's first station opened in 1847. The junction for the Coventry line opened in 1850. This station was a modest affair. Regarded as a second-class station on the Trent Valley Railway, within forty years its traffic would outstrip all others on the TVR line, and within thirty years it would be replaced on this site by the largest station on the line. (*Author's Collection*)

Right: An internal view of the first Nuneaton station when these platforms served main line, Leicester and Coventry line trains. (*Nuneaton Library*)

Nuneaton's second Trent Valley line station. The Coventry line bay was to the right, with the Burton on Trent, Ashby & Nuneaton joint bay to the left. There were no through roads on Platforms 1 and 2. The photograph was taken *c.* 1900. This station was rebuilt from 1913 onwards and these buildings entirely demolished to make way for the present station. The horse bus in this view was saved by the author and his friends from an allotment just south of Nuneaton. It was in remarkably good condition. It plied between the station and the Bull Hotel, which was the LNWR designated parcels office and overnight accommodation in the town. (*Author's Collection*)

The first ballast train to traverse the entire length of the Nuneaton to Coventry line travelled along it on 1 February 1850. Several months later the new line was ready and opened in its entirety to both passengers and freight on 2 September 1850.

Later, Midland Railway goods trains commenced to work over the LNWR branch between Nuneaton and Coventry under running powers granted by the Nuneaton and Hinckley Railway Act of 1860.

Nuneaton (Trent Valley Station) Coventry Bay Lines

When the new Trent Valley station opened at Nuneaton, it was a simple two-track affair, with a picturesque suite of traditional buildings in the Jacobean style designed by the LNWR architect J. W. Livock. Opening of the Coventry line followed by the South Leicester branch put pressure on the capacity of the station and a new island platform was built in the period 1868/69. The former Livock building was superseded by new main concourse buildings on the north side of the station in the 1870s. This new arrangement incorporated bays at each end: the south end for Coventry line trains and the north end for Ashby and Nuneaton line trains. The revised system worked well for some years, but the increasing volume of traffic through Nuneaton just before the First World War required these bay lines to be disposed of by putting a set of tracks through the station in their place to allow through running and ease congestion. Work on the new station meant that the former set of buildings needed to be replaced and they were demolished from 1913 onwards. Due to the outbreak of the war, work slowed and was not completed until 1915.

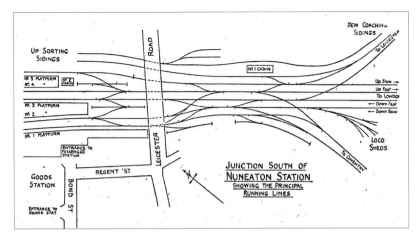

The layout at the south end of Nuneaton station, *c.* 1910 (*Railway Magazine*)

For a few years before the Second World War, Michelin rail cars were used on the Nuneaton, Coventry & Leamington service. They closely resembled the French railcars that were so typical after the war on French secondary railways. But this was a home-grown production. By 1935 Michelin were producing these railcars for the French market. Armstrong Siddeley obtained a concession to build a railcar from Michelin for the UK. The company saw it as a potential new market for its engines, gearboxes and transmissions. The bodywork was crafted in Nuneaton at the Midland Sheet Metal Co. at Chilvers Coton, and the wheels had rubber tyres made by Michelin that were to be a feature of the Paris metro system in later years. It proved very popular because it afforded excellent forward views, as you can see, but how it performed in everyday service does not seem to have been recorded, although there are records of trials carried out on the LNWR main line between Bletchley and London. The driver sat in a conning tower on top, rather like the French Picasso rail cars of later years. It was all very Gallic and a great novelty in its day. The car could take fifty-six passengers in some comfort, but there were technical disadvantages. For a start, it was very quiet due to the rubber tyres, which were fitted to reduce wheel noise and increase passenger comfort, and the track men called it the 'Silent Death'. Another problem with these early railcars was perceived lack of flexibility compared with steam trains. In the event of additional capacity being required, they could not attach an additional coach. There was no provision for attaching a parcels van. It seems the war put paid to the experiment, as passenger services reverted to trusted steam engines. Whatever became of the railcars and how they were disposed of is unknown, as the records do not seem to be available. (*Gordon Coltas*)

LMS 0-4-4T 41902 on the Nuneaton, Coventry & Leamington service at Nuneaton station in 1956–58 on a typical Coventry motor train. Full details of this loco's allocation to Warwick shed can be found with a picture of this engine at Coventry later in the book. Unlike the Michelin railcars, additional coaches and vans could be attached and at times of heavy loadings, trains like this ran with coaches in front and at the back of the engine or five-coach trains substituted. These engines appeared from time to time in the late 1950s, 41902 and 41909 being allocated for a short time at Warwick shed. This one was built at Derby in 1932 and withdrawn in 1959. (*Author's Collection*)

A two-car Metro Cammell DMU on the 4.15 p.m. ex-Leamington service enters Platform 1 at Nuneaton station on 11 March 1961. The Leicester Road Bridge is beyond and Nuneaton timber yard is behind the wall on the right with its distinctive crane. It is hard to reconcile a two-car DMU and the former five or more coach steam trains of the old days. Maybe passengers were driven away by being herded like cattle into the confines of a two-coach DMU after the spaciousness of the old steam trains, despite the modernity of the diesel units. Perhaps it's no wonder people deserted the railway in the 1960s due to the reduction in seating capacity and overcrowding forced people onto the buses. (*Mike Mensing*)

Above: A smoky departure from Platform 1 around 1960 with a Derby-built twin-car DMU on a Leamington train. A Nuneaton marshalling yard hump can just be seen off to the right with the extensive yards beyond. The remains of the goods yard are now occupied by the new Platforms 6 and 7 at Nuneaton station. (*Author's Collection*)

Right: A set of small signals were used to control engines moving from Platform 2 to go out main line, or using the short refuge road to park up between trains, as can be seen here around 1934. A 5-foot 6-inch tank is reposing in the engine release siding. (*E. H. C. Shorto*)

Below right: Extensive work is underway re-signalling Nuneaton station and the 'Coventry Bay Line' seen here in the mid-1960s. The old mechanical signals are just about to be phased out and new colour lights are in position. (*Author's Collection*)

Left: Looking towards the junction of the Coventry line with the Trent Valley lines with the former LNWR signals, which guided the local trains into the station, *c.* 1933. (*E. H. C. Shorto*)

Below: Nuneaton No. 2 Down Homes. At the same time as the previous picture, you can see the Coventry line access to Nuneaton station with the Webb 5-foot 6-inch tank in the engine release siding. To the right of the bridge abutment, you can see the hump used for marshalling trains in the extensive yards alongside the station. Coming off the Coventry line with its junction to the Trent Valley line, these LNWR pattern signals directed trains to Platforms 1 or 2, or out onto the main line, *c.* 1933. (*E. H. C. Shorto*)

Nuneaton's First Locomotive Depot

In 1850, a cottage industry began in Nuneaton – a small locomotive shed was erected and brought into use. It was equipped with two or three old-fashioned steam engines for working the brand new branch line to Coventry. It was a modest affair, employing just a few men, and survived little altered for the next twenty-eight years. The locomotive establishment at Nuneaton station would later become a major employer in the town, with over 400 members of staff. But that was many years in the future. In 1850, this quiet backwater was a rural idyll hidden amongst the miry lanes and green fields on the outskirts of town.

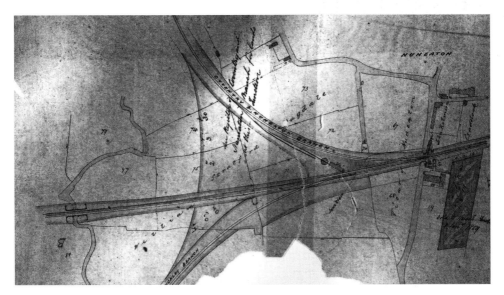

The line traversing left to right is the Trent Valley Railway from Rugby (left) to Stafford (right), as it approaches Nuneaton station, which is just off the plan to the right. The TVR opened in 1847. The Coventry branch goes off towards the top of the plan and opened in 1850. Leaving the TVR to the bottom of the plan is the South Leicester branch, heading towards Hinckley, the original section of which terminated at Hinckley in 1862. It was then extended through to a junction with the Midland Railway at Wigston in 1864. The original plan, which was an ink drawing on very thin tracing paper, must have been made c. 1862, as it refers to the Hinckley branch only, without mentioning its through route to Leicester, opened two years later. On the right is a level crossing, which stood where the foot tunnelnow connects Oaston Road and the top of Wheat Street. The foot tunnel is also shown on this plan. On the right, just below the road crossing, is the rectangular outline of a silk-ribbon factory, destroyed in a fire in the late 1960s. Where Nuneaton No. 1 signal box latterly stood until the end of steam, a small cabin stood controlling a level crossing, and when there were no trains passing the gates were open to let a few townsfolk through to reach the Oaston fields. The need for the box and the crossing was dispensed with when the Leicester Road Bridge was constructed in 1872. A new signal cabin was erected to replace this one and to carry out the increasing number of train movements on the main line. At the same time, another level crossing, which took the main Nuneaton to Hinckley road, was removed next to the station. These modifications coincided with tripling the Trent Valley main line. (*Author's Collection*)

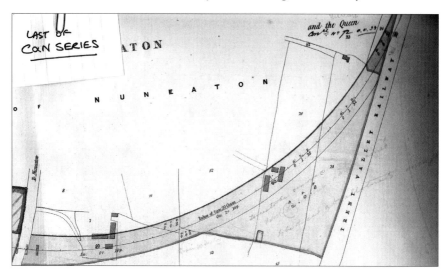

The original construction plan from 1850 and this section of the LNWR Coventry–Nuneaton branch shows the land purchase for the line as it approaches the Trent Valley Railway running into Nuneaton station. Two sets of structures are indicated on the track bed of the Coventry line. The accompanying section to go with the plan shows these are brickyards. The nearby clay pits from which the brick clay was obtained were adjacent to the line. The triangular section on the right was purchased for the site of the locomotive shed. (*British Railways, Estates Department, Euston*)

This second plan was prepared between 1864, when the Hinckley Branch was extended and became the South Leicester (shire) line, and 1873 when the Ashby & Nuneaton Joint line included a loop that ran from the trackage at the bottom of this diagram to the South Leicester at the top. There has been a modification to the shed sidings between the two diagrams. On the right at the bottom is the new Cotton Mill, opened in 1858 to provide employment for local people after the collapse of the silk trade in the preceding decade. The manufacture of silk ribbons was once the staple trade of the Nuneaton area, employing 60 per cent of the local population. This trade had been in decline since the 1830s. Increased activity in the local collieries, brickyards and quarrying had not provided sufficient work since then and the town had been in recession, despite opening the new railway. (*Author's Collection*)

Locomotive Facilities

The need for a locomotive to be stationed and serviced at Nuneaton was established in 1850 when the Coventry to Nuneaton route was opened. The branch engine was provided with a single-road engine house, located at the junction of the line with the Trent Valley main line in the vee of the two sets of tracks as they converged. The shed was equipped with a 35-foot-diameter turntable in front, which had to be negotiated to gain entrance to the building. No photographs of the structure are known to survive, but from later evidence it appears to have been timber built. Construction of timber sheds of that period indicate that they were erected on low brick walls with a slate roof and a smoke vent (or a series of small smoke vents) running along the apex of the roof. It was a simple affair.

When choosing a site for the shed, the LNWR cleared some ground that had been previously used as an old clay field. The area had gained the peculiar name 'Fudgy Nutt's'. The ground was soft clay of a 'fudgy' consistency and had, at one time, been occupied by a local ancient family of some status in the town by the name of 'Nutt'. This site would prove to be difficult for the railway's operational people thereafter because of its marshy substrate. Even as late as the 1960s, the much enlarged locomotive depot yard at Nuneaton was subject to settlement and soft ground. Keeping the shed yard track work in good order and alignment was a perennial problem. It may have contributed to the curtailed operational life of this shed, as it is known to have seen periods of non-usage in the 1860s and 1870s. Soft ground could possibly have caused misalignment of the 35-foot 0-inch turntable when first installed. When a new turntable was erected it made the shed itself useable again.

On 12 April 1855, the chief mechanical engineer of the Southern Division of the LNWR at that time, Mr J. E. McConnell, produced a list of allocations of engines at various steam sheds up and down the system. Nuneaton was allocated three engines: two in steam daily and one spare. These were used mostly for local traffic on the Coventry line. It seems two engines were enough for Coventry line work, one for passenger traffic and another for goods, shunting the various station goods yards and colliery exchange sidings, whereas Trent Valley line workings were carried out using Rugby or Stafford based engines.

In 1862, the Hinckley branch opened and this was extended two years later to Leicester via Wigston in 1864. Mr G. P. Neele, the traffic superintendent of the LNWR, recorded in his memoirs that he decided to extend the use of the Coventry & Nuneaton engine to work the traffic on the new line. Neele wrote:

The close of the year added a small extra mileage to the Central District viz. the first portion of the South Leicestershire line from Nuneaton to Hinckley four miles: a scheme has been submitted by Mr. Bruyeres for working the line with a separate engine. In conference at Euston I had considered that I could work it by extending the trips of the Coventry and Nuneaton service and avoid an extra engine; the idea exactly fitted the chairman's notions and the new line, which opened on 1 January 1862 was added to the Central District.

In a LNWR locomotive committee minute book entry dated 12 October 1866, the chief mechanical engineer, John Ramsbottom, noted a list of engines stationed at each station. There were none recorded at Nuneaton. It seems likely that the shed was out of service at that date for the reasons mentioned.

By 1870, the contractor widening the Trent Valley main line from two to three tracks at Nuneaton, William Moss of Stafford, asked if he could rent it for twelve months as a store, and as the locomotive department had no use for the place, the facility was granted for a rent of £2 per month.

A fondly remembered old timer with an encyclopaedic interest in old railways, who lived in Nuneaton, told me that William Moss used a decrepit old locomotive for his contracting work locally, known by the unofficial title 'Moss's Bug'. Presumably he

Although we cannot be entirely sure, there is circumstantial evidence to support this as being a loco based on Nuneaton's first engine shed. It is photographed at Hinckley station on the newly opened South Leicester branch, which led from Nuneaton to Wigston (then with running powers to Leicester over the Midland Railway main line) and opened in 1864. It was reported that the South Leicester line was worked by this type of rebuild in the 1860s and 1870s. The engine was old No. 21, built for the Birkenhead, Lancashire & Cheshire Junction Railway by Sharp Stewart (works No. 777 of 1851/52), which entered service on that railway in April 1854. It was acquired by the LNWR on 20 November 1860, when they acquired the interests of the BL&C and then numbered it 316, giving it the name *Prince Eugene*. The name was removed in 1862, and in 1868 it was rebuilt as a saddle tank in the form seen here. It looks to be in good external condition, so this view might have been taken shortly after conversion. Certainly the photograph was taken before April 1874 when the engine was renumbered in the duplicate list as No. 1821. This old-fashioned contraption was finally scrapped in September 1877. The train of primitive wooden coaches was a pretty typical rake of that period. The loco's duties may have involved working both to Coventry and to Leicester, possibly using the same rolling stock for both the Coventry and Leicester services. (*Edward Houlston, Hinckley, Gordon Webster Collection*)

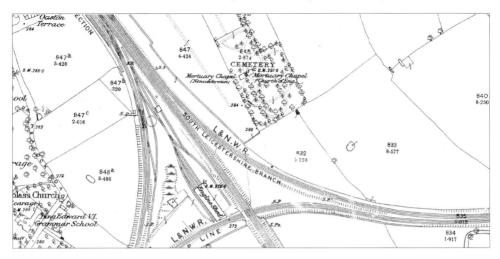

The 1887 Ordnance Survey map illustrates the 'new engine shed' erected in 1878: a four-road affair based on a standard LNWR Webb pattern northlight roof structure. The new shed would soon be extended (1888) to increase capacity up to eight roads, filling up the space between the four-road building and the Trent Valley main line. It clearly shows the marshy or 'fudgy' character of the former site with a small remnant enclosed within the triangle of lines adjacent to and to the left of the shed. The shed yard incorporates part of the old clay pit. In the centre of the map, Nuneaton Cemetery also occupied the remains of an old clay pit, and the depression in the centre where wreaths are laid today is a fragment of the clay hole. By this time, the loop line at the rear of the shed had been laid but was not much if at all used. This trackage was part of the Ashby & Nuneaton joint scheme, a joint venture between the LNWR and the Midland Railway that saw two sets of rails laid but soon mothballed through lack of use. It seems these were concessions provided for the Midland Railway's benefit and were insisted on by them to help move the A&N Construction Act through Parliament. One loop was laid alongside the Ashby Canal, which was then owned by the Midland Railway, who had it in mind to close the canal and divert their coal traffic emanating from the coal pits in the Leicestershire coalfield from a junction at Stoke Golding to another adjacent to Nutts Lane, Hinckley, with a junction on the LNWR South Leicester line facing towards Leicester. The loop at the rear of Nuneaton loco shed was also put in and equipped with a signal box at the Coventry line end controlling movements off and on the loop. The South Leicester end was controlled by what was later to be known as Midland Junction box. It soon dawned on the railway authorities that these loops were of no real practical use for traffic purposes, and when the LNWR became entirely responsible for the track at the southern end of the Ashby & Nuneaton joint, they lost no time in reducing their rateable value by severing them as through roads. The loop at the back of the shed did survive for many years, however, right up until the end of the shed in 1966. It was used for loco coal storage and, during the Second World War, the turntable was repositioned at the rear of the shed yard and coupled up to the loop to allow engines to escape from the shed yard in the Leicester direction, cutting down some of the complications when the shed yard was filled to capacity with locos. Sometimes the shed yard became so full of engines that they had to be parked in sidings around the station in order to wait their turn for using the shed, watering, coaling, maintenance and turning facilities. The loop line saw renewed importance during the war, and remained in constant use until closure to steam in June 1966.

kept it in the shed yard at Nuneaton and it became familiar to local railway enthusiasts in the 1870s. According to official LNWR records, William Moss purchased several second-hand locos for contracting work from them although, we do not know which ones he used for his Trent Valley widening contract in the 1870s.

On 8 October 1874, an official minute was recorded by Mr Cawkwell in the LNWR locomotive depot minute books that he proposed to use the shed at this station, which had not been used for some time, reducing the time engines were in steam. To do this the old 35-foot 0-inch turntable was to be replaced by a new 42-foot 0-inch one. The estimated cost of £280 was approved.

On 5 October 1877, Mr F. Webb, the chief mechanical engineer, submitted a plan to entirely rebuild the steam shed at Nuneaton station. However, the cost of demolition was fortuitously saved when a tremendous gale on 15 September 1878 blew the old wooden shed down. Two engines in the building were largely unscathed, despite being smothered by roof slates, timber beams and bricks, indicating the very lightweight construction of the shed. No one was in the building at the time, so thankfully there were no injuries reported.

EARLY LOCOMOTIVE ALLOCATIONS TO NUNEATON

Year	Loco No.	Type & Wheel Arrangement	Primary Service	Additional Notes/ Source
1860s	316	Sharp Single converted to saddle tank 2-2-2, but acquired second hand from the Birkenhead, Lancashire & Cheshire Junction Railway in November 1860	Nuneaton–Leicester branch	Photograph extant, taken by E. Houlston in the 1860s, rescued by Gordon Webster.
1870s	1913 (duplicate list)	Sharp Single converted to saddle tank 2-2-2	Nuneaton–Leicester branch	Other locos of this type were also allocated to Nuneaton for this service. (Source: *Chronicles of Boulton's Sidings*, Alfred Rosling Bennett)
1877–80	615 *Lune*	McConnell 'Small Bloomer' 2-2-2	Nuneaton–Leicester branch	Also used occasionally on the Ashby–Nuneaton service. (Source: *The Railway Magazine*)
Ditto	717 *Swift*	Ditto	Ditto	Ditto
Ditto	978 *Mammoth*	Ditto	Ditto	Ditto

COVENTRY & NUNEATON LINE PASSENGER TIMETABLE JANUARY 1876
(WORKED AS A LEICESTER THROUGH SERVICE)

Coventry to Leicester via Nuneaton

Leave	Monday–Saturday									Sunday	
	a.m.	a.m.	a.m.	a.m.	p.m.	p.m.	p.m.	p.m.	p.m.	a.m.	p.m.
Coventry	6.50	8.15	9.20	10.10	12.10	2.55	4.50	6.45	8.25	9.35	9.20
Coundon Road	6.55	8.20	9.23		12.15	3.00	4.55	6.50	8.30	9.40	9.25
Foleshill	6.59	8.24	9.29		12.20	3.04	4.59	6.54	8.34	9.45	9.30
Longford & Exhall	7.02	8.27		10.18	12.25	3.07	5.02	6.57	8.37	9.50	9.35
Hawkesbury Lane	7.05	8.30	9.33		12.29	3.10	5.05	7.00	8.40	9.54	9.39
Bedworth	7.10	8.35	9.38	10.24	12.34	3.15	5.10	7.05	8.45	9.59	9.44
Chilvers Coton	7.15	8.40		10.30	12.40	3.20	5.15	7.10	8.50	10.05	9.50
Nuneaton arrive	7.20	8.45	9.45	10.35	12.45	3.25	5.20	7.15	8.55	10.10	9.55
Hinckley	8.09	9.09		10.54	1.20	3.39	6.19	8.34	9.09	10.21	10.09
Elmesthorpe	8.16	9.16		11.16	1.28	3.46	6.25		9.21	10.31	10.16
Narborough	8.26	9.26		11.26	1.37	3.56	6.36		9.31	10.41	10.29
Blaby	8.31	9.31		11.31	1.44	4.01			9.36	10.46	10.35
Leicester	8.45	9.45		11.45	1.58	4.15	6.55		9.50	11.00	10.45

Leicester to Nuneaton and Coventry

Leave	Monday–Saturday									Sunday	
	a.m.	a.m.	a.m.	a.m.	p.m.	p.m.	p.m.	p.m.	p.m.	a.m.	p.m.
Leicester	6.45	8.50	10.35	11.40	3.10		4.40	6.25	8.15	7.40	5.45
Blaby		8.59	10.45	11.50	3.20		4.45	6.35	8.25	7.50	5.55
Narborough		9.04	10.50	11.55	3.25		4.50	6.40	8.30	7.55	6.00
Elmesthorpe		9.22		12.13	3.45		5.00	6.50	8.40	8.05	6.10
Hinckley	7.11	9.37	11.05	12.18	3.49		5.15	7.00	8.50	8.15	6.20
Nuneaton depart	7.50	9.40	11.35	1.16	4.00	5.00	6.00	8.30	9.05	8.30	6.40
Chilvers Coton	7.54	9.44	11.39	1.19	4.04	5.04		8.34		8.34	6.44
Bedworth	7.59	9.49	11.44	1.24	4.09	5.09	6.08	8.39	9.13	8.41	6.51
Hawkesbury Lane	8.04	9.54	11.49	1.29	4.14	5.14		8.44		8.45	6.55
Longford & Exhall	8.07	9.57	11.52	1.32	4.17	5.17		8.47	9.18	8.48	6.58
Foleshill	8.10	10.00	11.55	1.35	4.20	5.20		8.50	9.21	8.54	7.04
Coundon Road	8.14	10.04	11.59	1.39	4.24	5.24	6.17	8.54	9.25	9.00	7.10
Coventry	8.20	10.10	12.05	1.45	4.30	5.30	6.22	9.00	9.30	9.05	7.15

Nuneaton Loco Shed In Later Years

LOCOMOTIVE ALLOCATIONS AT NUNEATON SHED, 9 NOVEMBER 1912 (NO. 4 SHED ON THE LNWR AROUND 1885 ONWARDS– 1935)

Class	LNWR loco No./Name	LMS No.	BR No.	Date Withdrawn	Notes
6' 0" 2-4-0 Whitworth/ Samson Class	814 *Henrietta*	5082		July 1928	
4' 4" 0-6-0T	2633	(2)7508		March 1936	Ex-North London Railway.
5' 6" 2-4-2T	697	6690		March 1947	
	897	6617		September 1932	
	1157	6672		November 1934	
	1423	6746		September 1946	
	1762	(6634) not applied		May 1925	
	2134	6658	46658	December 1950	At Nuneaton in 1926, 1939 and 1945.
4' 6" 2-4-2T	5	(6539) not applied		January 1927	
	1192			1913	
	2067	(6574) not applied		April 1926	
5' 0" 4-6-0 'Bill Bailey' type	363			December 1914	
5' 0" 4-6-0 (19 inch goods)	2110	8798		1933	
	2601	8770		May 1936	
18" Goods 0-6-0	38	(2)8512	58396	June 1948	
	147	(2)8343		December 1947	
	397	8475		1931	

	422	8545		May 1934	
	774	(2)8610		June 1947	
	912	8378		1932	
	1130	8621		1932	
	2365	(2)8333	58363	April 1951	At Nuneaton in 1939 & 1945.
	2464	8334		1931	
Special DX 0-6-0	3041	(8008) not applied		March 1925	
	3050			March 1918	
	3072	(8065) not applied		May 1925	
	3081			March 1913	
	3097	(8032) not applied		February 1926	
	3149			December 1922	
	3314			October 1919	
	3551	(8085) not applied		July 1925	
Coal Engine 0-6-0	96	(2)8295	(58356) not applied	November 1948	At Nuneaton in 1945.
	153			1917	
	1179			1917	
	1320	8275		December 1933	
	2042	(8292) not applied		1924	
	2170	(2)8129		February 1946	
	2195	8109		1932	
	2381			1917	
	2397	(2)8202	(58339) not applied	May 1948	
	2426	(2)8240		?	
Compound B 0-8-0	1041	9355	49355	November 1959	
	1242	9388	(49388) not applied	March 1951	
	1547	8946		June 1928	
Compound C 0-8-0	1805	8959		December 1930	
	1814	8960		December 1930	

	2541	8953	48953	October 1961	
	2549	8963		December 1930	
	1849	(8987) not applied		February 1928	
	1867	8973		May 1933	
Compound 'E'	1017	(9605) not applied		October 1927	
	1064	8894	(48894) not applied	January 1949	
	1883	9319	(49319) not applied	October 1950	
Superheated G1 0-8-0	1162	9170	(49170)	June 1949	
	2001	9162	49162	May 1953	
	2015	9163	49163	December 1951	
Coal Tank 0-6-2T	180	7841		February 1948	
	1031	7806		March 1936	
Special Tank 0-6-0ST	1071	7298		December 1932	
	1422			?	
0-8-2T	1494	7875	(47875) not applied	August 1948	For hump shunting, Nuneaton marshalling yard.

NUNEATON LOCO SHED ALLOCATIONS

1935–37/1950, shed code 2D; 7/1950–9/1963, shed code 2B; 9/1963–6/1966, shed code 5E. 1948, 1950 until 1966. (Closure of Nuneaton MPD on 6 June 1966.) Additional information courtesy of Alan Cook, Mike Kimber and Ray Fox.

Class	Wheel Arrangement	No.	Allocation Dates	Notes (wdn = withdrawn from service)
3MT	2-6-2T	40003	10/1953–5/1954	wdn 1–2/1961
3MT	2-6-2T	40010	5/1960–3/1961	Shed Pilot wdn 7–9/1961
3MT	2-6-2T	40018	1948	wdn 8/1961
3MT	2-6-2T	40047	7/1952–11/1952	wdn 11/1959
3MT	2-6-2T	40049	7/1952–1/1958	wdn 7–9/1961
3MT	2-6-2T	40051	6/1960–3/1961	wdn 4/1961 from Nuneaton
3MT	2-6-2T	40053	7/1952–9/1952	wdn 8/1961
3MT	2-6-2T	40066	7/1952–9/1952	wdn 11/1959
3MT	2-6-2T	40068	7/1952–10/1952	wdn 12/1959
3MT	2-6-2T	40073	5/1955–6/1956	wdn 8/1962

3MT	2-6-2T	40077	2–5/1960	wdn 7/1961
3MT	2-6-2T	40081	2–3/1960	wdn 10/1961
3MT	2-6-2T	40087	10/1952–11/1960	wdn 11/1962
3MT	2-6-2T	40093	1/1953–4/1953	wdn 12/1962
3MT	2-6-2T	40104	11/1953–7/1956 10/1956–5/1961	wdn 9/1962
3MT	2-6-2T	40109	10/1952–9/1954	wdn 7/1962
3MT	2-6-2T	40122	10/1956–3/1957	wdn 6/1962
3MT	2-6-2T	40129	2–3/1960	wdn 10/1962
3MT	2-6-2T	40135	9/1952–11/1954 9/1958–10/1962	wdn 11/1962
3MT	2-6-2T	40137	10/1950–5/1952	wdn 11/1962
3MT	2-6-2T	40138	10/1956–1/1962	wdn 9/1962
3MT	2-6-2T	40143	1948, 9–11/1952	wdn 10/1961
3MT	2-6-2T	40156	11/1956–2/1957	wdn 10/1961
3MT	2-6-2T	40157	9/1956–6/1958 9/1958–7/1960	wdn 11/1962
3MT	2-6-2T	40180	3/1960–4/1960	wdn 1/1962
3MT	2-6-2T	40185	11/1959–3/1960	wdn 1–2/1962
3MT	2-6-2T	40201	1948–1/1951	wdn 7/1962
3MT	2-6-2T	40202	1948–7/1952	wdn 9/1962
3MT	2-6-2T	40204	1948, 2/1953–10/1959	wdn 11/1959
3MT	2-6-2T	40205	1948–4/1953	wdn 11/1962
3MT	2-6-2T	40206	1948	wdn 2/1962
3MT	2-6-2T	40207	3/1956–2/1961	wdn 2/1962
3MT	2-6-2T	40208	1948–10/1950	wdn 10/1961
2P	4-4-0	40413	1950–8/1952	wdn 1/1958
2P	4-4-0	40430	1948	wdn 4/1952
2P	4-4-0	40433	1948	wdn 10/1957
2P	4-4-0	40438	1950–6/1952	wdn 8/1954
2P	4-4-0	40447	1948, 1950–8/1952	wdn 5/1958
2P	4-4-0	40464	1948	wdn 7/1958
2P	4-4-0	40508	1948, 1950–5/1951	wdn 7/1951
2P	4-4-0	40528	1950–11/1952	wdn 12/1952
2P	4-4-0	40583	9/1952–1/1954	wdn 8–10/1960
2P	4-4-0	40589	1/1952	wdn 11–12/1959
2P	4-4-0	40676	7/1951–1/1954	wdn 11–12/1959
2P	4-4-0	40677	6/1952–1/1954	wdn 11–12/1959
2P	4-4-0	40683	1/1953	wdn 2–3/1961
2MT	2-6-2T	41211	8/1953–1/1955	wdn 8–9/1966
2MT	2-6-2T	41213	8/1953–1/1955	wdn 12/1963
2MT	2-6-2T	41226	7/1956–10/1958	wdn 9/1964
2MT	2-6-2T	41230	2–3/1955	wdn 3–4/1967
2MT	2-6-2T	41231	9/1955–5/1956	wdn 5/1966
2MT	2-6-2T	41234	1950–12/1950?	wdn 11/1966
2MT	2-6-2T	41235	1950–12/1952	wdn 11/1962
2MT	2-6-2T	41236	1950–6/1952	wdn 10/1962
2MT	2-6-2T	41237	1950–5/1952	wdn 9/1964
2MT	2-6-2T	41238	1950–6/1962	wdn 4/1965
2MT	2-6-2T	41239	2–5/1952	wdn 6/1964

2MT	2-6-2T	41244	7/1955–5/1956	wdn 11/1966
2MT	2-6-2T	41322	6/1956–10/1958	wdn 5–6/1964
2MT	2-6-2T	41323	6/1956–10/1958	wdn 5–6/1964
6P5F	2-6-0	42772	11/1960	wdn 5–6/1964
6P5F	2-6-0	42773	11/1961–5/1962	wdn 11/1962
6P5F	2-6-0	42777	1948, 1950–8/1953	wdn 8/1965
6P5F	2-6-0	42781	1948, 1950–8/1961	wdn 11/1962
6P5F	2-6-0	42783	1948, 1950–5/1962	wdn 8/1965
6P5F	2-6-0	42786	11/1961–5/1962	wdn 10/1962
6P5F	2-6-0	42810	6/1953–10/1954	wdn 12/1963
6P5F	2-6-0	42811	8/1959–5/1962 (or –2/1960?)	wdn 7/1962
6P5F	2-6-0	42813	1950–8/1953	wdn 11/1963
6P5F	2-6-0	42814	1948 still at Nuneaton 12/1960	wdn 8/1965
6P5F	2-6-0	42817	1/1951–10/1959	wdn 4/1965
6P5F	2-6-0	42849	5/1962	wdn 7/1965
6P5F	2-6-0	42851	12/1951–8/1952	wdn 7/1964
6P5F	2-6-0	42852	1951–2/1955 3–5/1955	wdn 7/1963
6P5F	2-6-0	42853	8/1959–5/1961	wdn 6/1963
6P5F	2-6-0	42854	12/1951– 1/1958 –5/1962	wdn 11/1963
6P5F	2-6-0	42859	3–5/1962	wdn 12/1966
6P5F	2-6-0	42885	2–5/1962	wdn 12/1963
6P5F	2-6-0	42886	5/1962	wdn 4/1965
6P5F	2-6-0	42888	1948, 1950–10/1954	wdn 2/1964
6P5F	2-6-0	42891	1/1951–1/1960	wdn 10/1962
6P5F	2-6-0	42924	11/1960	wdn 2/1966
6P5F	2-6-0	42925	11/1960	wdn 11/1964
6P5F	2-6-0	42926	6/1959–8/1961	wdn 10/1964
6P5F	2-6-0	42932	1948, 1950–9/1952	wdn 5/1965
6P5F	2-6-0	42933	1950–9/1952 8/1959 –8/1961	wdn 5/1963
6P5F	2-6-0	42935	8/1959 3–5/1962	wdn 1/1962
6P5F	2-6-0	42939	8/1959–5/1962	wdn 6/1962
6P5F	2-6-0	42941	1948, 1950–9/1952 5/1962	wdn 5/1965
6P5F	2-6-0	42944	1950–8/1955 11/1960 4–5/1962	wdn 4/1963
6P5F	2-6-0	42945	9/1961–11/1964	wdn 3/1966
6P5F	2-6-0	42946	6/1962–10/1964	wdn 11/1965
6P5F	2-6-0	42947	6/1962–5/1963	wdn 11/1965
6P5F	2-6-0	42950	6/1962–5/1963	wdn 10/1965
6P5F	2-6-0	42951	4/1953–5/1953	wdn 10/1965
6P5F	2-6-0	42953	1/1961–10/1962	wdn 1/1966
6P5F	2-6-0	42954	9/1961–5/1963 12/1963–7/1964	wdn 2/1967
6P5F	2-6-0	42956	6/1962–5/1963	wdn 9/1964
6P5F	2-6-0	42958	1948, 6/1962–5/1963	wdn 11/1965
6P5F	2-6-0	42959	1948	wdn 12/1965

6P5F	2-6-0	42960	8/1950 9/1961–5/1963	wdn 1/1966
6P5F	2-6-0	42962	6/1962–12/1963	wdn 2/1964
6P5F	2-6-0	42964	10/1954–1/1955 –5/1963	wdn 11/1965
6P5F	2-6-0	42965	9/1961–11/1962	wdn 8/1964
6P5F	2-6-0	42967	6/1962–12/1964	wdn 5/1966
6P5F	2-6-0	42968	6/1962–5/1963	wdn 12/1966
6P5F	2-6-0	42969	6/1962–5/1963	wdn 12/1964
6P5F	2-6-0	42970	6/1962–5/1963	wdn 10/1964
6P5F	2-6-0	42971	6/1962–5/1963	wdn 12/1964
6P5F	2-6-0	42973	6/1962–10/1963	wdn 11/1963
6P5F	2-6-0	42975	1/1961–4/1963	wdn 3/1966
6P5F	2-6-0	42976	9/1961–12/1961	wdn 7/1963
6P5F	2-6-0	42977	1/1961	wdn 6/1966
6P5F	2-6-0	42978	1/1961–9/1963	wdn 5/1966
6P5F	2-6-0	42980	5/1963	wdn 1/1966
6P5F	2-6-0	42981	6/1962–5/1963	wdn 5/1966
6P5F	2-6-0	42982	6/1962–12/1963	wdn 11/1965
7MT	2-6-0	43000	11/1957–3/1961	wdn 9/1967
4MT	2-6-0	43001	1/1951–? 11/1957–9/1962	wdn 9/1967
4MT	2-6-0	43002	9/1953–9/1962	wdn 12/1967
4MT	2-6-0	43003	9/1953–4/1955 7/1958– 9/1962	wdn 9/1967
4MT	2-6-0	43005	8/1961	wdn 11/1965
4MT	2-6-0	43006	9/1953–3/1955 6/1958–9/1962	wdn 3/1968
4MT	2-6-0	43007	6/1958–5/1962	wdn 9/1967
4MT	2-6-0	43009	6–8/1960	wdn 12/1966
4MT	2-6-0	43011	3/1951–3/1957	wdn 2/1967
4MT	2-6-0	43020	8/1950 3/1958–9/1962	wdn 10/1966
4MT	2-6-0	43021	8/1950 2–5/1962	wdn 9/1967
4MT	2-6-0	43022	8/1950 6/1959–9/1962	wdn 12/1966
4MT	2-6-0	43023	8/1950 1950–3/1960	wdn 12/1967
4MT	2-6-0	43024	8/1950 11/1957 –9/1962	wdn 6/1967
4MT	2-6-0	43025	8/1950	wdn 9/1965
4MT	2-6-0	43026	12/1958	wdn 9/1966
4MT	2-6-0	43027	11/1950–3/1951	wdn 5/1968
4MT	2-6-0	43034	11/1954–12/1954 also during 60s	wdn 6/1967
4MT	2-6-0	43052	10/1959–8/1960 2–5/1962	wdn 10/1966
4MT	2-6-0	43112	2–5/1962	wdn 9/1967
4MT	2-6-0	43113	2–9/1962	wdn 9/1966
4MT	2-6-0	43115	2–5/1962	wdn 6/1967
3F	0-6-0	43308	12/1956–1/1957	wdn 10/1959
3F	0-6-0	43786	10/1952–9/1957	wdn 10–11/1957
4F	0-6-0	44239	5/1960	wdn 10–11/1963
4F	0-6-0	44593	10/1957–3/1958	wdn 11–12/1963
5MT	4-6-0	44771	6/1965–6/1966	wdn 3/1967

5MT	4-6-0	44831	6/1965–6/1966	wdn 11/1967
5MT	4-6-0	44866	6/1965–6/1966	wdn 9/1967
5MT	4-6-0	45001	6/1965–6/1966	wdn 3/1968
5MT	4-6-0	45056	3/1964–8/1964	wdn 8/1967
5MT	4-6-0	45065	6/1965–6/1966	wdn 5/1968
5MT	4-6-0	45310	6/1965–6/1966	wdn 8/1968
5MT	4-6-0	45405	6/1965–6/1966	wdn 8/1967
5MT	4-6-0	45448	6/1965–6/1966	wdn 8/1967
6P5F	4-6-0	45533	12/1960–8/1961	wdn 1962
6P5F	4-6-0	45537	12/1960–4/1962	wdn 1962
6P5F	4-6-0	45538	7/1962	wdn 1962
6P5F	4-6-0	45541	12/1960–4/1962	wdn 1962
6P5F	4-6-0	45542	7/1961–4/1962	wdn 1962
6P5F	4-6-0	45548	1–4/1962	wdn 1962
6P5F	4-6-0	45599	10/1961–1/1963 5/1963–6/1964	wdn 9/1964
6P5F	4-6-0	45603	11/1961–11/1962	wdn 12/1962
6P5F	4-6-0	45624	11/1961	wdn 11/1963 (stored at Coventry loco depot – depot then closed – 11/1963–3/1964)
6P5F	4-6-0	45643	12/1962	wdn 11/1963
6P5F	4-6-0	45669	10/1961	wdn 5/1963
6P5F	4-6-0	45723	10–12/1962	wdn 9/1964
6P5F	4-6-0	45724	7–9/1962	wdn 10/1962
2MT	2-6-0	46420	12/1960–1/1965	wdn 1/1965
2MT	2-6-0	46446	11/1958–12/1958	wdn 12/1966
2MT	2-6-0	46447	9/1961–4/1961	wdn 12/1966 preserved at Quainton Road railway preservation site.
2MT	2-6-0	46495	5/1963–5/1966	wdn 10/1966
3F	0-6-0T	47285	1948, 1950–4/1959	wdn 7–9/1965
3F	0-6-0T	47286	1948, 1950–2/1957	wdn 7–9/1965
3F	0-6-0T	47294	2/1960–6/1962	wdn 10–11/1963
3F	0-6-0T	47367	1958, 1950–4/1956	wdn 11–12/1966
3F	0-6-0T	47385	6/1961–5/1962	wdn 3–5/1964
3F	0-6-0T	47396	6/1961–2/1963	wdn 10–11/1966
3F	0-6-0T	47478	5/1963–2/1964	wdn 3–5/1964
3F	0-6-0T	47491	10/1956	wdn 12/1962
3F	0-6-0T	47594	1948, 1950–4/1959	wdn 5–7/1964
8F	2-8-0	48016	1950–8/1963	Ex-WD engine 70591 wdn 11/1965
8F	2-8-0	48020	1950–8/1963	Ex-WD engine 70579 wdn 8/1965
8F	2-8-0	48054	6/1960–4/1966	wdn 9/1967
8F	2-8-0	48074	6/1960–6/1962	wdn 11/1967
8F	2-8-0	48077	1950–6/1962	Ex-WD engine 70611 wdn 3/1968
8F	2-8-0	48111	8/1959–5/1966	wdn 3/1968
8F	2-8-0	48154	9/1954–7/1962	wdn 7/1967
8F	2-8-0	48251	4/1959–2/1964	wdn 10/1966

8F	2-8-0	48258	9/1956–6/1962	Ex-WD engine 70398 wdn 8/1967
8F	2-8-0	48263	8/1959–5/1966	Ex-WD engine 506 wdn 9/1966
8F	2-8-0	48264	6/1960–5/1966	wdn 7/1966
8F	2-8-0	48287	8/1959–6/1962	Ex-WD 70402 wdn 6/1967
8F	2-8-0	48289	8/1959–5/1966	Ex-WD 70413 wdn 10/1966
8F	2-8-0	48312	11/1954–6/1962	wdn 2/1965
8F	2-8-0	48320	9/1952–5/1966	wdn 3/1967
8F	2-8-0	48326	5/1962	wdn 7/1966
8F	2-8-0	48343	7/1953–1/1966	wdn 2/1967
8F	2-8-0	48345	1950–5/1959	wdn 3/1968
8F	2-8-0	48365	5–6/1962	wdn 5/1968
8F	2-8-0	48372	7/1953–2/1958	wdn 12/1966
8F	2-8-0	48398	2/1956–after 1960	wdn 4/1966
8F	2-8-0	48435	1950–6/1962	wdn 5/1967
8F	2-8-0	48449	1950–8/1963	wdn 5/1967
8F	2-8-0	48456	1950–5/1966	wdn 8/1967
8F	2-8-0	48479	1–4/1953	wdn 2/1966
8F	2-8-0	48504	8/1959–4/1966	wdn 6/1968
8F	2-8-0	48526	1950–8/1958 ?–6/1962	wdn 9/1966
8F	2-8-0	48623	7/1957–10/1964	wdn 10/1966
8F	2-8-0	48658	1/1954–6/1962	wdn 7/1965
8F	2-8-0	48686	2/1956–5/1966	wdn 11/1966
8F	2-8-0	48716	1950–9/1958	wdn 8/1965
8F	2-8-0	48723	1950–6/1963	wdn 8/1968
8F	2-8-0	48751	9/1953–5/1966	wdn 2/1967
8F	2-8-0	48753	6/1960–4/1966	wdn 3/1967
8F	2-8-0	48754	2/1960–6/1962	wdn 6/1967
7F	0-8-0	48896	1948	wdn 1/1950
7F	0-8-0	48911	1948	wdn 12/1949
7F	0-8-0	48927	1950–12/1959	wdn 11/1961
7F	0-8-0	49002	4/1951–12/1960	wdn 9/1962
7F	0-8-0	49045	2–4/1962	wdn 12/1962
7F	0-8-0	49068	1948, 1950–12/1956	wdn 1/1957
7F	0-8-0	49079	11/1959–4/1962	wdn 11/1962
7F	0-8-0	49080	1948	wdn 2/1950
7F	0-8-0	49082	1948	wdn 10/1960
7F	0-8-0	49112	10/1952–10/1959	wdn 11/1959
7F	0-8-0	49114	1948	wdn 11/1962
7F	0-8-0	49120	9/1954–7/1959	wdn 9/1959
7F	0-8-0	49134	11/1959–12/1960	wdn 3/1962
7F	0-8-0	49142	2/1953–12/1960	wdn 12/1962
7F	0-8-0	49144	9/1957–12/1959	wdn 11/1962
7F	0-8-0	49150	1948	wdn 11/1959
7F	0-8-0	49172	8/1951–5/1957	wdn 8/1957
7F	0-8-0	49181	1948, 1950–2/1959	wdn 4/1959
7F	0-8-0	49190	1948	wdn 2/1950

7F	0-8-0	49191	1948	wdn 10/1961
7F	0-8-0	49212	2–9/1951 12/1951 –2/1956	wdn 4/1956
7F	0-8-0	49264	1948	wdn 1/1951
7F	0-8-0	49268	1948	wdn 11/1959
7F	0-8-0	49270	11/1958–10/1959	wdn 11/1959
7F	0-8-0	49293	9/1950–4/1962	wdn 11/1962
7F	0-8-0	49304	1950–7/1954	wdn 12/1959
7F	0-8-0	49314	3/1955–5/1962	wdn 11/1962
7F	0-8-0	49318	1948, 1950–5/1953	wdn 11/1957
7F	0-8-0	49339	1950–11/1954	wdn 12/1954
7F	0-8-0	49342	1948, 10/1952–9/1961	wdn 10/1961
7F	0-8-0	49345	1948	wdn 1/1958
7F	0-8-0	49346	1948	wdn 5/1952
7F	0-8-0	49350	1948, 1950–4/1962	wdn 12/1962
7F	0-8-0	49351	1948	wdn 11/1949
7F	0-8-0	49352	1948	wdn 9/1962
7F	0-8-0	49366	1948	wdn 10/1959
7F	0-8-0	49368	1950–11/1951	wdn 1959
7F	0-8-0	49377	3/1955–2/1956	wdn 10/1962
7F	0-8-0	49385	1950–5/1951	wdn 12/1957
7F	0-8-0	49396	8/1950–8/1950	wdn 11/1959
7F	0-8-0	49397	1950–1952	wdn 11/1959
7F	0-8-0	49400	1948	wdn 11/1959
7F	0-8-0	49412	1948	wdn 10/1961
7F	0-8-0	49414	1950–8/1961	wdn 10/1961
7F	0-8-0	49415	11/1958–1960/61	wdn 11/1962
7F	0-8-0	49424	1950–5/1956	wdn 9/1962
7F	0-8-0	49425	11/1958–4/1962	wdn 9/1962
7F	0-8-0	49428	1948	wdn 12/1962
7F	0-8-0	49430	1948, 8/1951–3/1957 5/1957–8/1960	wdn 12/1964
7F	0-8-0	49431	11/1958–4/1962	wdn 11/1962
7F	0-8-0	49432	1948, 1950–12/1960	wdn 11/1962
7F	0-8-0	49434	1949–1950	wdn 10/1962
7F	0-8-0	49435	1948	wdn 11/1959
7F	0-8-0	49436	1948	wdn 5/1959
7F	0-8-0	49437	1948, 1950–11/1951	wdn 9/1962
7F	0-8-0	49439	1948	wdn 12/1962
7F	0-8-0	49440	3/1958–1/1962	wdn 3/1962
7F	0-8-0	49441	11/1958–8/1961	wdn 10/1961
7F	0-8-0	49453	1950–3/1952	wdn 10/1961
7F	0-6-0	52107	1948	wdn 3/1953
3F	0-6-0	52141	1948, 1950–11/1956	wdn 5/1960
3F	0-6-0	12294 (52294) not applied	1948	wdn 8/1949
3F	0-6-0	52321	1948	wdn 2/1954
3F	0-6-0	52322	1948, 1950–7/1952	wdn 8/1960

3F	0-6-0	52429	1950–9/1954	wdn 9/1960
3F	0-6-0	52465	1950–4/1955	wdn 6/1955
2F	0-6-0	58116	1948	wdn 1/1960
2F	0-6-0	58118	1948, 1950–12/1958	wdn 1/1960
2F	0-6-0	58240	1948 1950–3/1953	wdn from Nuneaton, wdn 5/1953
2F	0-6-0	58272	10/1950–3/1954	wdn. 5/1954
2F	0-6-0	58281	6/1954–12/1958	wdn 4–5/1959
2F	0-6-0	28333 (58363) not applied	1948	wdn 4/1951
2F	0-6-0	58368	1948	wdn 6/1951
2F	0-6-0	28532 (58405) not applied	1948	wdn 7/1948
2F	0-6-0	58426	1948	wdn 10/1952
5MT	4-6-0	73004	1–5/1965	wdn 10–11/1967
5MT	4-6-0	73032	7/1964–4/1965	wdn 8–9/1965
5MT	4-6-0	73033	3–6/1965	wdn 1/1968
5MT	4-6-0	73045	9/1964–4/1965	wdn 7–8/1967
5MT	4-6-0	73073	7/1964–6/1966	wdn 10–11/1967
5MT	4-6-0	73159	9/1964–6/1965	wdn 10–11/1967
4MT	4-6-0	75010	10/1962–2/1963	wdn 10–11/1967
4MT	4-6-0	75011	10/1962–4/1963	wdn 10/1966
4MT	4-6-0	75012	10/1962–2/1963	wdn 1/1967
4MT	4-6-0	75016	5/1963–5/1965	wdn 6/7 1967
4MT	4-6-0	75018	5/1963–4/1966	wdn 5–7/1967
4MT	4-6-0	75032	10/1962–4/1963 7–1964	wdn 2/1968
4MT	4-6-0	75033	10/1962–4/1963	wdn 12/1967
4MT	4-6-0	75034	10–11/1962	wdn 2/1968
4MT	4-6-0	75035	10/1962–5/1963	wdn 7–8/1967
4MT	4-6-0	75045	5/1963–2/1966	wdn 4/1966
4MT	4-6-0	75050	10/1962–4/1963	wdn 11/1966
4MT	4-6-0	75052	1/1963	wdn 4/1967
4MT	4-6-0	75063	5/1963	wdn 6–7/1966
4MT	4-6-0	76020	5/1959	wdn 5/1966
2MT	2-6-0	78018	10/1965–3/1966	wdn 11/1966
2MT	2-6-0	78039	10/1965–4/1966	wdn 11/1966
2MT	2-6-0	78059	10/1965–6/1966	wdn 11/1966 The last loco on Nuneaton shed. Left end of June 1966 after removal of shed stores. Is now preserved on the Bluebell line.
3MT	2-6-2T	82020	10/1954–10/1956	wdn 9/1965
3MT	2-6-2T	82021	10/54–10/1956	wdn 10/1965

Above: Bog standard motive power on the Coventry and Leamington services for over sixty years were these primitive, simple and sturdy old locomotives, the Webb 2-4-2T. No. 781 is standing in Nuneaton shed yard between duties around the early 1920s, post grouping, although it had not lost its LNWR number at that stage. Old Nuneaton drivers have told me that these were strong engines, with excellent free-steaming qualities and a good turn of speed, but they were cramped and uncomfortable to work on in the confined space of the cab. The big problem was that the side tanks extended back to the footplate door, as you can see here, and a balancing pipe for these tanks passed through the doorway, obstructing it. Therefore you could not stand in the doorway for refuge. It was particularly awkward if the driver was rather fat, as his hapless fireman, standing in very close proximity, had to swing his shovel from the bunker to the fire hole door without coming into bodily contact with his rotund mate. A lurch caused by a bad joint in the track could cause the fireman in such awkward circumstances to lose his balance and the coal was scattered over the footplate, much to the disgust of the driver – some drivers were martinets prone to lurid language. Sometimes it did not augur well for a fireman marked with a Webb 2-4-2T and a certain driver, because it was going to be a long and miserable day. An old driver told me that one of his mates, who regularly drove these tank engines, was a miserable cuss to work with, but as soon as he was taken off the Webb engines and he had a new Stanier or Ivatt 2-6-2T with their spacious and comfortable cabs his personality changed overnight. He became almost a charming fellow, relaxed and amiable thereafter. No. 781 entered service in June 1889 and was renumbered 6581 by the LMS in September 1927, finally being withdrawn in March 1930. (*Author's Collection*)

Opposite above: Ex LNWR 'Experiment' 4-6-0 No. 5491 *Prince George* started life as LNWR No. 1135 in September 1907, was renumbered as we see here by the LMS in March 1927, and withdrawn in June 1934. 5620 alongside it was a Prince of Wales class of loco. Originally No. 2198 *John Ruskin*, it entered service in November 1913 and was withdrawn in March 1936. The photograph was taken on 24 October 1933. (*J. M. Bentley Collection*)

Opposite below: Nuneaton shed yard sees former LNWR 'Experiment' LMS No. 5461 *City of London* on 15 October 1932. It entered service in February 1906 and was withdrawn in May 1934. (*W. L. Good*)

Ex-LNWR 19-inch goods 4-6-0 No. 8799 rests on Nuneaton depot with a well loaded tender on 15 October 1932. (*J. M. Bentley Collection*)

Another view of 5461 at Nuneaton, with a rare glimpse of the old turntable pit that stood in front of the shed. The turntable here was replaced and moved to the back of the shed during the Second World War to enable larger engines to be handled and facilitate access to the table from two directions to speed up release of engines, 15 October 1932. (*J. M. Bentley Collection*)

Ex-LNWR 5-foot 6-inch 2-4-2T No. 6660 off duty at the side of the shed. This engine never made it into BR days. Built in 1893, it was withdrawn in September 1947. (*J. M. Bentley Collection*)

8488 started life as LNWR 18-inch Goods 0-6-0 No. 1743, which entered service in May 1899 and was then renumbered by the LMS in September 1928. It was rebuilt with a Belpair firebox in March 1926, and withdrawn in 1932. (*Gordon Coltas*)

G2A (or Super D) ex-LNWR 7F 0-8-0 No. 49115 is turned on the 'new' turntable installed during the Second World War at the rear of the shed. In the background you can see the large mill that was owned by Fielding Johnsons. 49115 was a 'foreign' engine at this time. Built in 1910, it was withdrawn in November 1959. One of the cast-iron turntable plates from this turntable has been preserved in private ownership. (*A. G. Ellis*)

2P 4-4-0s, such as 40683 seen here, were regularly used on Coventry/Leamington line services up until the 1950s. 40683 was shedded at Nuneaton in 1953. 40683 was built in 1932 and withdrawn in 1961.

The combined effect of sulphurous smoke and water vapour affected all of the old cast-iron Webb saw-tooth roof or northlight sheds to various degrees of decrepitude. Many sheds were rebuilt in the 1950s when the old roof was taken down, and a new steel roof installed. To keep the shed in use, it was reroofed in two halves. I guess this photograph was taken on a Sunday when the shed was full. (*Author's Collection*)

Ex-MR 0-6-0 No. 58281 was a regular engine on the Abbey Street line and on the Coventry line. It was at Nuneaton between June 1954 and December 1958. The loco was put into service in 1897 and withdrawn from service in May 1959. (*Maurice Billington*)

The LMS-built 0-6-0 4Fs, such as 44259, were not liked by Nuneaton men; as a result we did not have many. They were fitted with inadequate MR-designed axle boxes, which ran hot, and some crews said they were poor steamers too. There was banter between former North Western men and Midland men on this subject. Nevertheless they were produced in great numbers, but it is significant that only a very few were allocated to Nuneaton. No. 44259 was built at Derby and entered service in 1926 and was withdrawn in 1964. It bears a 17D (Rowsley) shed plate and was a fair distance from home. (*Author's Collection*)

Class 3MT 2-6-2T No. 40207 was a regular engine at Nuneaton for five years, being allocated between March 1956 and February 1961. These were replacements for the old Webb 5-foot 6-inch tanks. A 'D' reposes to the right. The shed roof has not yet been rebuilt. 40207 was at Coventry depot when withdrawn in February 1962, and was scrapped by Cashmores, Great Bridge in November 1962. (*Author's Collection*)

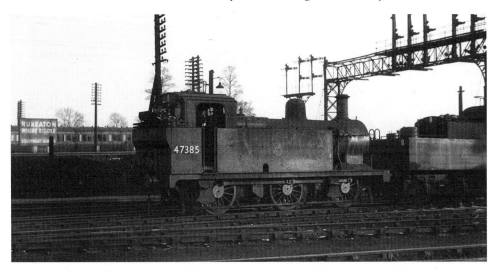

This loco is a 'Dobbin' not a 'Jinty', and various enginemen at Nuneaton shed could get very upset if the weasel word 'Jinty' was mentioned. These 3F LMS-built 0-6-0Ts were mostly used on north end freight yard shunting and shed pilot duties at Nuneaton, dragging out locos and repositioning them as the despatch roster of motive power was sorted out. No. 47385 was only allocated to Nuneaton for twelve months between June 1961 and May 1962. No. 47385 was one of a batch of these locos built by Vulcan Foundry, which entered service in 1926 and was withdrawn in 1964. Nuneaton's carriage sidings can be seen across from the main line in the background. As these were adjacent to Nuneaton's municipal cemetery, they were known to railwaymen as 'Cemetery Sidings' or less tastefully 'The Bone Yard'. (*Author's Collection*)

41231 was one of the regular class of 2MT 2-6-2Ts on the Coventry/Leamington passenger services, but was only at Nuneaton a short time between September 1955 and May 1956. Others of its class lasted longer. This type of loco, together with its tender engine equivalent, the 464XX series were great favourites of local enginemen due to the comfort of the footplate. No. 41231 was built in 1949 at Crewe, and was last shedded at Leamington, being withdrawn from there in May 1964. It was scrapped by Cashmores, Great Bridge, in August 1964. (During 1954 two auto fitted 2-6-2Ts, Nos 41211 and 41213, were tested between Nuneaton and Leamington with a view to working certain workman's trains as auto-trains. An ancient motor coach, No. M3404, was used for these trials.) (*Author's Collection*)

3F 0-6-0T No. 47285 reposing on shed was a long time resident from 1950 until at least April 1959. It was built by the Hunslet Engine Co. in 1924 and lasted in service until 1965. (*Keith Lambourne*)

LMS 4F 0-6-0 No. 44597 moves off shed after 1963. Built at Derby, it entered service in 1940 and lasted until 1965. It must have been a foreign engine at the time, as there is no record of it being allocated here, certainly in BR days. (*Author's Collection*)

Nuneaton acquired over 50 per cent of this class of loco at one time or another. They were a common sight in the 1930s–1960s. A mass influx occurred in June 1962 as other sheds got rid of them and this was one. As the new diesel types came in, and DMUs took over passenger workings, a great many steam engines were cascading down to lesser duties, and this resulted in the Stanier design of 6P5F engine (known as 'Stanier Crabs') congregating at Nuneaton, where it can only be assumed there would be work for them, and the local shed crews were familiar with their idiosyncrasies. By this time the Super Ds were rapidly disappearing, but they were not liked by local enginemen for various reasons, and there was not enough work for them to go round. Local footplate crews had a meeting and told management that it was dangerous working on these locos under the wires as withdrawing the fire irons could bring the metalwork in contact with the catenary, with obvious results. The management agreed and the 'Stanier Crabs' were despatched mostly *en bloc* up north in 1963, where they continued in service for a few more months before the inevitable withdrawal from service. It can only be assumed that a small amount of work could be found for the remainder out of danger of contact with the overhead wiring until the last disappeared in 1964. No. 42967 was one of a batch built at Crewe in 1934 and was at Nuneaton between June 1962 and December 1964. Its last shed was Heaton Mersey, from where it was withdrawn in May 1966 and its cut date was November 1966 at Birds, Long Marston. (*Author's Collection*)

No. 48445 has a crudely painted 5E shed code in this view. This pins the date down to its allocation between June 1965 and June 1966 when the shed closed, and it was transferred to 10D (Lockstock Hall). It was withdrawn from there in May 1968 and scrapped by Wards of Beighton, Sheffield, the following September. No. 48445 had been built at Swindon and entered traffic in 1944. (*Author's Collection*)

Local enthusiasts and footplatemen alike were delighted when these engines turned up. No. 45537 is seen here in December 1960. They found modest employment on relief express passenger trains, the 'Blaby's', or Leicester goods working and some local passenger services, but their days were numbered when they got to Nuneaton although they were still in good condition and gave the fitters little trouble. No. 45537 was named *Private E. Sykes VC*. Built at Crewe in 1933, it was reallocated away from Nuneaton in April 1962 before being withdrawn in 1964. (*Maurice Billington*)

More superpower cascaded down from main line duties was this 'Jubilee' 4-6-0 No. 45586 *Mysore*, which found itself at Nuneaton, although not allocated here. Built by the North British in 1934, *Mysore* was withdrawn in 1965. (*Author's Collection*)

A Class 8F 2-8-0 in pretty work-worn condition, which was normal state towards the end of steam. Note the boarded crossing in the foreground. This is how the engine crews got to the shed (and generations of trespassing trainspotting shed bunkers). (*Author's Collection*)

No. 42331 a Fowler 2-6-4T was often
seen at Nuneaton, although none of this
class of engine were actually shedded here.
Electrification is underway as No. 42331
attached to an Ivatt Class 4 2-6-0 head
off down the Coventry line on a wintry
day. No. 42331 was withdrawn in 1962
having entered service in 1929 built at
Derby. Gantries for electrification wires
were erected for a short distance on to
the Coventry line for shunting purposes.
(*Author's Collection*)

To many of us youthful trainspotters,
No. 40087 was a famous 'wreck' as it stood
forlorn in the back lay by road at Nuneaton
shed for two years after it was taken out
of service. Built at Derby in 1935, it was
allocated to Nuneaton in October 1952
and could be seen on all the local passenger
services between then and November 1960;
then it went away for a short period until
it returned the following February to be
withdrawn (officially in November 1962),
but as far as I can remember after its return it
did not see much service and languished out
of use until towed away for scrapping in July
1963. I remember going onto the footplate
of this engine when it stood here, and seeing
the metal surfaces red with rust, and mould
growing on the timber floorboards. Not long
after it was towed away it was cut up at
Crewe that August. (*Author's Collection*)

Stanier 8F 2-8-0 No. 48085 keeps the
company of an unidentified 'Black Five'
at Nuneaton, probably in the period
1964–65 when it was a Northampton
engine. No. 48085 was built by Vulcan
Foundry, entered service in 1937 and was
withdrawn from Northwich in August
1967. It was later scrapped at Buttigeigs
scrapyard, Newport, in November 1967.
(*Mike Kinder*)

Standard types in view of the shed in 1965, when this photograph was taken, engineman's bothy and Coventry line in the foreground. The standard class of 4-6-0s in the 73 and 75 series were replaced by an allocation of Black Fives in 1965, which took over their dwindling duties. (*Author's Collection*)

During the hiatus period of 1963/64, when the wiring was energised from Crewe to Nuneaton, the loco shed was used to garage Type 4 diesels used to bring the trains north from Euston, hook off and be replaced by an electric at Nuneaton. A Type 4 is about to move off the shed to take over a southbound train. A DMU on a Leicester–Nuneaton train can just be seen to the left of the brick-built structure in the centre of the picture. Steam days are numbered. (*Author*)

As the role of the steam loco diminished generally and Nuneaton in particular, several quite modern locos such as these BR built Class 2MT 2-6-0s in the 78 series were mothballed. Nuneaton had Nos 78018, 78039 and 78059 until early 1966. It looks as though all three and another unidentified member of the class are out of use here during the winter of 1965/66 prior to despatch to Crewe. The last example, No. 78059, was steamed again in June to assist with the decommissioning the shed. Locomotive stores, oil and spare parts being collected up and loaded into trucks before despatch to Crewe. The shed closed on the evening of Sunday 6 June 1966. The withdrawal of steam engines locally meant that their remaining duties: Hawkesbury Junction – Longford Power Station – Coundon Road and Nuneaton–Websters sidings were dieselised, but these trip workings soon ceased. (*Mike Kinder*)

An overall view of the shed in around 1963. The triangular formation is clearly in view at this point, with Fielding Johnson's cotton mill on the far right. The former loop line between the Coventry line and the Leicester line can be seen, as well as the turntable, which allowed locos to leave the shed in the Leicester direction. (*Author's Collection*)

Above left: The last loco to remain at Nuneaton after the shed closed on 6 June 1966 was used for three weeks to clear up stores and take surplus material away. It left for Crewe afterwards. Here are the staff remaining at the shed on that fateful day after the other locos were sent away over the weekend. No. 78059 entered service in September 1956 and was withdrawn in November 1966. Happily it has survived, being rescued from Dai Woodham's famous railway scrapyard at Barry Island and going to the Bluebell Railway for preservation after sixteen years in the scrap line. The personnel lined up are: George Brookes, Edwin Holmes, Harry Gunn, Alan Burnham – all fitters; Mrs Randle, office clerk; Ernie Morris, office clerk; Jack Green, fitter; Don Foulds, driver; Bill Lowe, running shed foreman. On the footplate are Albert Harris, Alf Drake, drivers, and Charlie Woodford, fitter; George Hall, fitters mate kneeling. (*Charlie Woodford Collection*)

Above right: After the shed closed, weeds took over, but it stands here forlorn awaiting the demolition gang that reduced it to rubble between September and December 1968. The photograph was taken in October 1966. (*Author*)

Nuneaton Shed Loop

A loop line was put in at the rear of Nuneaton loco shed as part of various Ashby & Nuneaton sections, opened in 1873 as a loop built from Midland Junction box through to the Coventry line, which burrowed under the Trent Valley main line and completed the trackage around a triangle of land purchased by the LNWR in 1850.

The rear of the shed in October 1966, with an express hauled by an electric passing over the bridge, which carried the Trent Valley over the former loop line. The rails are still in place but heavily overgrown in this view and not visible after being out of use for over twelve months. (*Author*)

Fielding Johnson's Siding

The large mill we knew latterly as Fielding & Johnson's was originally built in the 1850s, primarily to bring work to the people of Nuneaton, which was suffering from the complete collapse of the silk ribbon industry that had been the staple trade of the district up until that time. It was originally a cotton mill and the siding was known to train staff right to the end of operations as 'The Cotton Hole Siding'. The siding was disused after 1948 when the two big steam engines at Fielding Johnson's, called *Annie* and *Elizabeth*, were dispensed with and the mill went over to electric power. Coal deliveries by rail were discontinued.

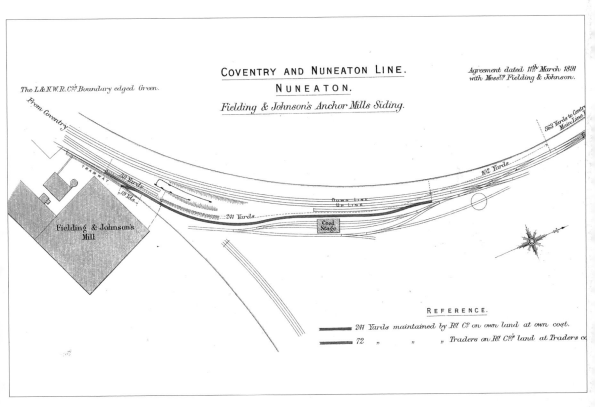

Fielding Johnson's factory. The 'Cotton Hole' siding was tucked away between the chimney and the retaining wall. The Coventry line traverses the picture from right to left (Attleborough Road passes under the bridge to the left of the mill). Delivery of coal over this siding ceased in 1948 when *Annie and Elizabeth*, Fielding & Johnson's magnificent steam engines, were dispensed with in favour of electrical power. I understand the siding remained in situ until the demolition of the loco shed in 1968. (*Author's Collection*)

Two class 20s on a stone train pass the cleared site of Fielding Johnson's factory as the area is prepared for the new housing that followed. (*Author*)

Cotton Hole Siding. Oops: a pile up at the end of the siding when several wagons were shunted on the steeply graded coal siding and got out of control. It ended in a big pile up at the bottom of the siding, probably in the 1920s. Workmen disentangle the mess. It looks as though the wagon on the left has overshot the manager's house garden and come to rest in his shrubbery. (*Courtesy Tom Burgoyne*)

Coton Arches

Between Nuneaton loco shed and Chilvers Coton, the line passed through open fields later to become Riversley Park. The stretch was graded at 1 in 126, so very often steam engines tackling this bank with a heavy mineral train put on a fine show for strollers in the park. Beyond the park, an impressive set of brick arches were built to carry the line over the Coventry Road. This has been known to generations of locals as 'Coton Arches' and they still stand today. The railway bridge was contracted to a local builder and bricks were brought from local Stockingford brickyards in carts at 350 bricks per load. One of the arches was let out to local businesses and Woods Garage was in business there from 1920 until the 1960s. Another occupant of the ground below the archway was Whitehall's, a bus firm who regularly took workers to the engineering factories in Coventry.

A panoramic view showing Coton Arches with the Coventry line passing over it. The land in the foreground has been built over since Geoff took this picture from the top of the bell tower at Coton Church in the mid-1960s. (*Geoff Edmands*)

A road view of Coton arches from Coton Road, possibly in the 1940s. Coton Road extends up to the bridge here and Coventry Road is beyond the bridge. Note the lack of traffic at a junction today which is very busy. (*Author's Collection*)

Chilvers Coton Station

In August 1881, the LNWR was being petitioned to provide better accommodation at Chilvers Coton station. There was no shelter on the Up platform and the waiting room was only sufficient to hold twelve people, but occasionally thirty to forty people were crammed into it. In the *Nuneaton Chronicle*, 20 January 1882, it was reported there was a fire at the station and the original wooden station was gutted. A temporary building was sent from Tamworth in the meantime. The *Nuneaton Chronicle* on 31 March 1882 reported again that a new station building was erected, which cost £500. Mr Whitcome of Stafford was the contractor. The last station was a typical LNWR standard wooden structure mass produced at Crewe.

By the 1930s, 900 tickets to Coventry were sold at Chilvers Coton station every day. There was a train every ten minutes. It cost *6d* to park your bike at Coton station per day, and two or three cottages offered daily bicycle storage services. If you had a puncture, you could tell the owner of the parking ground and he would repair it for you, at a nominal cost of course, and the bike was ready for you when you returned to cycle home.

A 2-car Park Royal DMU passing the closed Chilvers Coton station on Sunday 12 September 1965. This was a special shuttle service to carry passengers from the 5.40 p.m. Birmingham New Street to Rugby while electrification was taking place on the main line. (*Mike Mensing*)

Inset: Chilvers Coton station's award-winning Coronation garden. (*Ted Veasey Collection*)

Above right: The cheerful station staff at Chilvers Coton with their award-winning garden. Note the bricks forming the word Chilvers Coton painted in white. The names are (from left to right): Mr and Mrs William Ashley, Anne Royce and Eddie Bowler. (*Ted Veasey Collection*)

Right: Chilvers Coton station was the first stopping place on the way to Coventry from Nuneaton. The village of Chilvers Coton had once been a separate community and was amalgamated to become part of Nuneaton Urban District Council and the two parishes joined so that Chilvers Coton was swallowed up into the suburbs of Nuneaton. The totem here announced your arrival at the station in the 1960s (with the remnants of the fine gardens that won awards in their day). A general air of neglect fell on the station in this period. The end of the upkeep to the garden came about when BR time and motion study people turned up one day and thought the staff at the station had too much time on their hands if they had time to tend the garden between trains and cut the number of staff.

Below: Near Griff Junction during the last days of steam, a 9F No. 92247 heads towards Coventry with a freight. No. 92247 was a Banbury engine at this time. It was withdrawn in October 1966 and scrapped by Drapers of Hull in April 1967. 9Fs were never allocated to Nuneaton and could (only just) be turned on the local shed turntable. This train is probably taking coal back to Banbury to be interchanged with the Great Western Railway for distribution over that system. Nuneaton crews sometimes had Banbury workings as well for this purpose using their own engines.

Griff Junction

On 28 June 1877, the LNWR sought fresh powers to extend the Griff Branch (LNWR New Lines Act 40 & 41 Victoria, Chapter 44). The new line reused the original stub line of 1850 from the Griff Canal basin and extended to a terminus near what is now Westbury Road, Stockingford, although that road had not been built then. The Griff Branch opened on 22 July 1881. After the Griff Branch was lifted in October 1963, Griff Junction box remained as a fringe box for the Nuneaton power box on the Trent Valley main line. Griff Junction box closed in February 1985. A rather unusual arrangement was related to me by Vic Holloway, who arranged for me to visit to Griff box before it closed: the Coventry line signal linesmen, who were Rugby men, but based at Nuneaton, looked after the Coventry line from Griff Junction signal box to Coundon Road, then skipped Coventry and looked after the stretch from Gibbet Hill to Kenilworth Junction.

Inside Griff Junction box in the 1980s. (*Author*)

The Griff Extension Railway

The Griff Extension Railway, LNWR(New Railways) Act 1892 55 & 56 Victoria, Chapter 4, was proposed to run 6 furlongs 5 chains and 25 links to the Birmingham–Leicester line of the Midland Railway near Stockingford station, together with 2 miles 6 furlongs, 6 chains and 30 links from the head of the Griff Branch through the Haunchwood brickworks site to meet the Midland Railway's Stockingford branch near Stockingford Colliery. Neither of these extensions were built.

Griff Canal Arm Wharf

Right: Griff Junction signal box, looking towards Nuneaton, 30 March 1958. The bridge in the foreground crosses the Griff arm of the Coventry Canal. The canal arm was still busy with coal traffic right up until the closure of Griff Collieries. (*Geoff Edmands*)

Below: This bridge carried the Coventry line over the Griff Arm of the Coventry Canal. It is seen here on 9 March 1958.

Griff Collieries

Griff wagon, one of the thousands used by the colliery to deliver their products all over the South of England. This one was bought in, but others were built in the colliery workshops using a kit of metal parts supplied by outside suppliers. (*Historical Model Railway Society*)

Griff Pumping Station Siding

Two shafts 6 foot 0 inches in diameter were sunk purely as pumping shafts to reach the 2 yard slate and 7 feet seams for the purpose of trapping water which flooded through the old workings through outcrops. These drained pits from Whittleford to Bedworth. The shafts were called *Caroline* and *Barbara*, after two female members of the Newdigate family. They were fitted with Newcomen & Watt beam pumps (one of which dated back to at least 1780), which drained 33,600 gallons per hour, which they carried out economically for many years until being replaced about 1950 with electric submersible pumps. The pumping engines were provided by coal from a siding which led off the Griff Clara colliery branch at the Griff canal arm.

A very historic and well-known Griff loco was a 0-4-2T of extremely ancient lineage, which is believed to have originated on the London & Birmingham Railway around 1840. It displayed some Bury Curtis & Kennedy features (bar frames) but its real origins now seems to be in doubt. The St Helens Railway may be another contender for its early service. It was standing at Griff Colliery when purchased in 1911 for the Shropshire & Montgomeryshire Railway. It was probably acquired by Griff when the contractors who had completed the Ashby & Nuneaton line offered for sale various locos they had used on the construction work, but which were surplus to requirements. This would have been around 1873. After sale to the S&M, Crewe, as it was named at Griff, was overhauled by Bagnalls of Stafford. The loco became No. 2 Hecate on the S&M but was renamed Severn in 1915 or 1916. New brass nameplates were cast for it at the time. Severn was reported to have been scrapped in 1931, but this was only dismantlement because parts lay around for years at the S&M Kinnerley depot. When disposal was considered, an offer was received from Wards and Cohen, two scrap dealers, in 1930 but the GWR would not allow it to be taken away over their metals in such a decrepit state, so these offers were not taken up. In 1933 the boiler was sold to a firm in Wednesbury, and in 1937 a local firm dismantled the rest. The inside cylinders were 14½-inch diameter and set between bar frames. Round coupling rods connected the 4-foot 6-inch-diameter coupled wheels. The trailing wheels were 3-foot 6½-inch diameter. The total wheelbase was 13 feet 3 inches and the overall length 26 feet 3 inches. With 1,000 gallons of water the all up weight was 28 tons. The S&M purchased it through a locomotive dealer, Mr Hartley, in May 1911 from the Griff Collieries.

Inset: A great favourite at Griff despite its rather antiquated appearance, *Britannia* is seen here in the 1950s. An 0-6-0ST by Hunslet, it was later fitted with a spark arrestor on the chimney. It was scrapped on site by J. & H. B. Jackson Ltd scrap merchants of Coventry in September 1956. (*Maurice Billington*)

Success at Griff No. 4 pit on 16 April 1954 has been newly overhauled with a Perspex back to the formerly open cab. Note the coal stacked inside the cab, which looks positively dangerous should it lurch on a set of points and send those big lumps cascading on to the legs of the footplate crew. Also note the 'Chip Pan' spark arrestor. The closure of No. 4 pit on 22 July 1960 saw this engine transferred to Haunchwood Colliery with *Good Luck*. (*M. J. Lee*)

Griff's 0-6-0ST HE 498/1890 was out of steam in this view. After closure of the Griff Collieries it was sent to Haunchwood Colliery but did not see much work there (if any). (*Author's Collection*)

A short wheelbase made this loco ideal for the tighter corners on the Port of London Authority dock lines for which it was originally built, and it was probably useful for this reason on Griff's internal rail system, although the wheel loading might have been a problem with the lightly built trackwork in places. It arrived from the War Department in 1948 numbered 70211, which it kept throughout its short career and was repaired by Hudswell Clarke in 1954. It lay out of use for a while before being scrapped on site sometime after October 1960. (*M. J. Lee*)

LOCO LIVERIES

Bobs, *Britannia* and *Good Luck* were painted black with red lines, and had red wheels with black rims. *Success* was in the standard ex-Barclays livery of leaf-green, with yellow and black lining, green wheels with black rims.

Griff Collieries engineering depot made their own wagons at the pit using bought in metal parts and timber fabricated in their workshops. The journals were cast at the Chilvers Coton foundry. Wagon bolts were forged and machined at the colliery. The colliery internal tub line was 21-inch gauge and tubs were hauled by 'monkeys' on 'creepers'. The tub bodies were also made at Griff. Tub wheels came from Hadfields of Sheffield. The labour cost of putting two new tub wheels on the axles was 1s, and 3d was allowed for tightening the axle on.

LOCOMOTIVES AT GRIFF

Name/No.	Wheel/Cylinder Arrangement	Maker	Works No./ Date	Notes
Crewe	0-4-2ST IC	Bury Curtis & Kennedy	*c.* 1840	Ex-LNWR in the 1870s. Sold to the Shropshire & Montgomeryshire Railway in May 1911 by R. Hartley, dealer.

Swallow	0-4-0ST OC	Black Hawthorn	174/1873	Secondhand via C. D. Phillips, dealer, Newport, S. Wales, 1882. Rebuilt by William Bagnall, Stafford in 1894. Sold to Neville Druce & Co. Ltd, Llanelly, Carms. via William Cornforth & Co., Kidsgrove, Staffs, December 1901.
Knutsford	0-6-0T IC	Sharp Stewart	3471/1888	Ex-T. A. Walker, Manchester Ship Canal contract. Sold to Broughton and Plaspower Coal Co. Ltd, near Wrexham, Flint.
Britannia	0-6-0ST IC	Hunslet Engine Co.	222/1879	Ex-Alexandra (Newport & South Wales) Docks & Railway, Newport, Monday June 1894. Scrapped on site by J. & H. B. Jackson Ltd, September 1956.
Good Luck	0-6-0ST IC	Hunslet Engine Co.	498/1890	Purchased new. Repaired by S. Briggs & Co. Ltd, Burton on Trent, August 1952. Returned 9 July 1953 then sent to Haunchwood Colliery, September 1962.
Bobs	0-6-0ST IC	Manning Wardle	1102/1889	Ex-J. S. Jackson, dealer South Wales. Scrapped on site, April 1948.
Success	0-6-0ST OC	Andrew Barclay	1167/1909	Purchased new. To Haunchwood Colliery 21 December 1960.
Cowburn	0-4-0ST OC	Hunslet Engine	544/1891	Ex-Pooley Hall Colliery, January 1948. Returned to Pooley Hall June 1949.
WD No. 75010	0-6-0ST IC	Hunslet Engine	2859/1943	Ex-War Department, March 1948. To Baddesley Colliery, August 1948.
WD No. 70211	0-6-0T OC	Hudswell Clarke	1102/1915	Ex-War Department, 1948. To Hudswell Clarke, April 1954. Returned June 1954. Scrapped by John Cashmore Ltd (on site) sometime after October 1960.

Griff Coal, mostly steam and house coal, was transported over a wide area and reached almost as far as away as Exeter on the Great Western Main Line.

Griff Clara closed on 28 May 1955, although locomotives continued to work through to the colliery until September 1956 on land sale and coal wharf duties. By the end of 1956, most of the rails were lifted down to the Griff Canal wharf. Griff No. 4 Colliery closed on 22 July 1960. Lifting of the Griff Branch was completed by October 1963.

Haunchwood Brick & Tile
Nos 2 & 3 Yards

No. 1 yard was at Stockingford, therefore does not come within the scope of this book. No. 2 yard was in production by 1889, but may have been much older, and Haunchwood might have purchased one of the many small brickyards extant in the Heath End area in the nineteenth century and expanded its production. There was a rope-worked wagon way, which crossed Heath End Road on a bridge and dipped down into a clay hole on the opposite side of the road. This clayhole still exists and is known locally as the 'Blue Lagoon'. No. 2 yard made red facing bricks, common red bricks, chimney pots and quarry tiles. The yard closed in 1939. Some of the drying sheds were used for storage during the Second World War by the Ministry of Food as a buffer depot. Attempts to reopen the yard failed and the brick sheds and kilns stood derelict until demolition in the early 1970s.

No. 3 yard: again, this yard almost certainly reused earlier workings and was in production by 1889 at Bermuda making stoneware pipes, fittings, common bricks, hollow fire clay blocks and unglazed drain land drain pipes. The yard was expanded and a rope- or chain-worked tramway passed via a tunnel under Bermuda Road into a large clayhole. The trackwork was 2-foot 0-inch gauge and there are reports of a narrow gauge loco being used at one time but details are unknown. The yard closed 1969/70. The goodwill of the remaining Haunchwood business was taken over by Thomas Wragg of Swadlincote in 1970. Both yards were shunted by Griff Colliery locos by loose agreement with the colliery management. It is likely Griff also supplied the coal for the Haunchwood kilns and drying sheds, in view of the close proximity of the pit to the brickyard.

Stanley Brothers Ltd

Stanley Brothers took over a brickyard owned by Wheway & Handley on Nuneaton Common in the late 1860s and also worked a colliery close by called Nuneaton Colliery. For a short time they operated another very small coal pit known as Swan Lane colliery which was close to the brickyard, in the period 1872–78. Stanley's lobbied the LNWR for the extension of the short shunting stub to Griff collieries to reach their works and collieries and this new stretch of line opened in 1881. (For details see the introduction to the Griff Branch.) Stanley's had their own shunting locos:

Name/Running No.	Wheel/Cylinder Arrangement	Builder	Works No.	Dates Scrapped or Disposal
?	0-6-0ST IC	Hunslet Engine	499/1890	Ex-Appleby Iron Co. Ltd (No. 4) scrapped approx. 1927.
Sale	0-4-0ST OC	Hunslet Engine	263/1881	Ex-T. A. Walker, Manchester Ship Canal contract, 1896.
Florence	0-4-0ST OC	Manning Wardle	593/1877	Ex-Premier Cement Co. Ltd, Irthlingborough, Northants. It stood for some years after it ceased working about 1945 in No. 3 yard in Croft Road before being sold for scrap to J. & H. B. Jackson Ltd, Coventry, December 1950.
Ancoats	0-4-0ST OC	Manning Wardle	1091/1988	Ex-T. A. Walker, Manchester Ship Canal contract. Sold to Thos. E. Gray Ltd Refractory Manufacturers, Isebrook Quarry, Burton Latimer, 1922. Rebuilt in 1922 with Sentinel vertical boiler. Sold for scrap to W. J. Redden & Sons, Wellingborough, August 1956.
Westwood	0-4-0ST OC	Yorkshire Engine Co.	257/1975	Rebuilt by James Tait & Partners, their works No. 69/1920. It had earlier worked at the Frodingham Iron & Steel Co. Ltd, Appleby, Lincolnshire. It was sold in November 1961 to G. W. Bungey Ltd in November 1961 but never left the Stanley's site before being sold on in 1962 to George Cohen, Sons & Co. Ltd, Kingsbury, for scrap.

Ironsides	0-4-0ST	Henry Hughes		The origin of *Ironsides* is unknown, but it was probably built in the 1870s. After Charity Colliery, Bedworth, closed in 1925, it was transferred to Stanley Brothers' yards in Stockingford. It was later scrapped.
Norman	0-6-0ST IC	Manning Wardle	240/1867	This was also transferred from Charity Colliery in 1925 and sold for scrap at an unknown date.
	4W DM	Ruston Hornsby	299098/ 1950	Purchased new and effectively replacing the only steam loco then still working, *Westwood* was the last steamer to work here but its duties were taken over by the RH. Rail traffic by the 1950s was greatly reduced. It was sold to G. W. Bungey Ltd, dealer with *Westwood* in 1961, and was sold on to Sheepbridge Stokes Ltd, of Chesterfield, Derbyshire, and escaped the scrap merchant's torch.

The only photograph I have seen of a loco on the Griff branch, taken of No. 2936, a 'Crab' 6P5F 2-6-0 with driver Horace Beers on the footplate. It is standing on the branch near to Haunchwood No. 2 yard, paused in between shunting duties. These engines were very popular with Nuneaton crews, being strong with free-steaming boilers, and I have never heard a word against them. They were truly mixed traffic locos, good on freight and occasional passenger trains, particularly excursions to Blackpool or the North Wales coastal resorts. No. 2936 was built at Crewe in 1932 and was withdrawn from Birkenhead shed in July 1965 and scrapped by the Central Wagon Co., Ince, in August 1965. (*Courtesy Betty Melbourne*)

After the Griff branch was lifted and before the derelict brickyard buildings at Haunchwood Brick & Tile's No. 3 yard were cleared away, Geoff Edmands climbed the Griff No. 4 slag heap and took a series of panoramic views across the industrial wasteland at Bermuda. The track bed of the Griff branch can clearly be seen in this view where it widened to incorporate the colliery marshalling sidings.

The photographer, Geoff Edmands, has turned his camera and pointed it towards Heath End Road and the pit head buildings of Griff No. 4 Colliery. The raw cut of the Griff branch is to the left of the brickyard chimneys of Haunchwood No. 2 yard. Scattered across the picture are the various chimneys and brick sheds associated with Stanley Brothers workings, the Griff branch underbridge, where it traversed under Heath End Road to the extreme left and carried on towards Stanley Brothers sidings, ending up near Westbury Road. The rails had been taken up in 1963.

Stanley's loco *Florence* was used up until 1945 but was laid aside after the war as it was then thoroughly worn out. During the war it had seen relatively intensive service handling trucks for the Ministry of Food depot, which utilised some redundant kilns for buffer storage. The Daimler Co. also used old sheds in the brickyard for strategic storage during the war. *Florence* could be seen scuttling across the level crossing with trucks for these depots. It was originally built for the Burton Brewery Company Ltd as their No. 2 and was a standard Manning Wardle 'H' class of loco. She was cut up on site in December 1950 by Jackson & Co. Ltd, the Coventry scrap merchant. (*K. J. Cooper Industrial Railway Society Collection*)

William Griffiths Ltd

There has been extensive quarrying in this area of Nuneaton for 200 years and it is one of the few old industries to survive into the twenty-first century as stone is still quarried close to the Coventry–Nuneaton line. Workings on this site date back to the middle of the nineteenth century. A narrow gauge tramway was in position by 1902, which led to the Griff Canal arm at Bermuda for the loading of stone either into rail wagons or barges. A private siding agreement with the LNWR was entered into on 1 March 1912 at the same time as a new crushing and loading plant was installed. Another quarry face was opened up close by and the narrow gauge tramway (2-foot 6-inch gauge) was extended over the Coventry Road out of Nuneaton. A small diesel locomotive was purchased to work part of this line in 1950.

Name/No.	Wheel Arrangement/Type	Maker	Works No.	Notes
-	4w DM	Motor Rail	20024/1950	Purchased new in 1950. Disposed of by 1963.

The bridge that used to take the Williams Griffiths tramway over Coventry Road (Griff Hollows) is being dismantled. A fine selection of period cars are being routed to avoid the crane, whose outriggers encroach on the centre of the road. This scene has now been entirely eradicated by the new dual carriageway road and all signs of the bridge have disappeared without trace. (*Geoff Edmands*)

Bedworth Furnaces

Contractors for the furnaces were Addenbrooke, Pidcock & Co. The proprietors: were the Bedworth Charity Iron & Coal Company. Addenbrooke, Pidcock & Co. was a business started in 1840 in Darlaston where they were coal and ironmasters. This company took over ironstone working in the form of balls and nodules mined on the Nicholas Chamberlain Charity estate. Extensive blast furnaces commenced operations in November 1873. A celebratory dinner was laid on for 1,000 workmen at the national schools in Bedworth at that time. Some of the equipment came from the Roughay Works of Addenbrooke & Pidcock, Darlaston. Two smelting furnaces 50 feet 0 inches high were capable of producing 360 tons of pig iron per week. It was a short-lived affair, as official abandonment of workings of the black ironstone took place on 25 June 1877. By 1879 the furnaces were disused and stood cold and increasingly derelict until demolition took place in 1894. The reason the furnaces were uneconomic was that many of the uses to which wrought iron produced at Bedworth was being put were rapidly replaced by the manufacture of steel by the Bessemer process, which superseded high-grade iron for many industrial purposes.

The short branch to the furnaces was accessed from the Charity Colliery branch and terminated at a wharf on the Coventry canal. Shunting was carried out by Charity Colliery locos. *Chamberlain* No. 1 was new in 1873 and its arrival may be contemporary with the increased requirements of the new furnaces opened that year.

I am most grateful to John Burton for finding this photograph because I am sure it is of Bedworth Furnaces and was taken by Clare Speight, a local photographer in Nuneaton when the furnace was in the early stages of demolition in 1894. There are certainly signs that the structure is to be demolished, with preparation work started around the base of one of the smelting furnace structures. Broken windows indicate that vandalism was prevalent in Bedworth even back then, as this had stood unused for seventeen years, having received its last charge of local iron in 1877. The wagons may have been brought in to take away scrap metal liberated by the demolition. (*Clare Speight, John Burton Collection*)

Charity Colliery

The mineral rights were owned by the Nicholas Chamberlain Charity. Lessees included: Peter Unger Williams until his death in 1837 and Caroline Williams (widow of the former until 1858). The colliery was offered for sale by auction in August 1861. Their sons, John McTaggart Williams and Charles McTaggart Williams, were trading as Williams Brothers until 1861, George Barker & Sons, later as Bedworth Coal & Iron. Ltd (1878–96), Stanley Brothers Ltd (1899–1924) by Leasehold for £450 per annum from 20 April 1899. The lease was given up on 20 April 1925.

A horse-drawn tramway from the colliery to the Coventry Canal was operated until 1835. The colliery line to the LNWR branch was opened in 1850. New exchange sidings for the Charity Colliery line were put in 1883.

During the Stanley Brothers' lease they provided hundreds of standard coal wagons to deliver the coal which had large white letters on the side reading 'Bedworth'. In 1915 this amounted to 446 wagons valued at £13,437 5s 4d. In 1915, all five locos were written down in Stanley Brothers books, to the value of £458 17s 1d.

Name/Running No.	Wheel/Cylinder Arrangement	Builder	Works No.	Disposal Details
Chamberlain No. 1	0-4-0ST OC 12x18"	Manning Wardle	439/1873 (New)	Sold to Topham Jones & Railton Ltd contractors, 1918.
Ironsides No. 2	0-4-0ST OC	Henry Hughes & Co.		Transferred to Stockingford Works in 1925.
Norman No. 3	0-6-0ST IC	Manning Wardle	240/1867 (New)	Transferred to Stockingford Works in 1925.
Glenmayne No. 4	0-4-0ST OC	Peckett	P983/1904 (New)	Sold to Haunchwood Brick & Tile Co., Stockingford, 1925.
Forest No. 1	0-4-0ST OC	Peckett	484/1889	Ex-Upper Forest & Worcester Steel & Tinplate Works Ltd, via dealer J. F. Wake, Darlington, in 1909. Disposal, subsequent use and scrapping details are unknown.

The mineral rights to Charity Colliery were owned by the Nicholas Chamberlain Charity in Bedworth. There are ten known separate shafts on the Charity estate. Charity No. 1 colliery opened in 1776. This closed around 1830. In the same year another colliery was established at Collycroft, No. 2 colliery, which was sunk to alleviate poverty in the silk ribbon industry, which was badly affecting Bedworth at that time. This colliery employed thirty-eight men and eight boys in 1841. There was also a brickyard on the site, and when operated by the Bedworth Coal & Iron Co. Ltd in 1878 it had a capacity of 100,000 bricks per week. Only two shafts were being worked by 1879. The colliery's official closure date was 13 September 1924.

Bedworth Brick Tile & Timber Co. Ltd

This siding was built by agreement with the LNWR, dated 30 June 1900. Adjacent to Bedworth station, the official LNWR above may have been preceded by other agreements since the site was worked as a colliery at an earlier date. Brick production had ceased by 1920 although the siding was in situ for another thirty years.

Bedworth Station

A new signal box was erected at Bedworth station in December 1876. Bedworth station, like all the stations on the Nuneaton, Coventry & Leamington line, did a very brisk trade. All types of goods were handled in the goods shed. Fish, poultry, livestock and huge quantities of beer were brought in fresh daily. Bedworth won several best-kept station awards, and for some years the name Bedworth was laid out in whitewashed bricks surrounded by a picturesque garden. One of the best-remembered stationmasters was Wilfred Foskett, who was a well known local character.

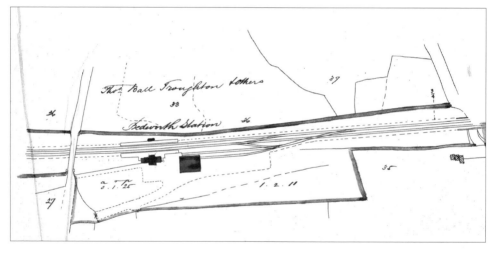

Above and left: The old station at Bedworth was replaced during the first few years of the twentieth century by a much larger building on both platforms as passenger traffic increased. On the right is a brickyard that also had a number of coal shafts associated with it at one time. (*D. B. Mole, Bedworth*)

Geoff Edmands took a series of photographs of Bedworth station and they stand the test of time as a comprehensive record of this well-built, robust structure with all the usual offices and appurtenances of a busy commuter station. This is the entrance lobby as you descended from Bedworth street level down to the station. Closure was only two months away when these photographs were taken in January 1965.

Inset: Bedworth station staff at the old station before the Second World War. (*Bedworth Echo*)

The growing town of Bedworth with its numerous brickyards and collieries as well as local workpeople in close commuting distance to the car factories of Coventry made good use of its station. The photograph was taken on 2 January 1965. Geoff's car is in the foreground. (*Geoff Edmands*)

Another view of Bedworth station trackside on 2 January 1965, looking towards Coventry. (*Geoff Edmands*)

Looking towards Coventry in January 1965; a general view of Bedworth station with the goods yard on the left. (*Geoff Edmands*)

Inset: The goods being handled here is a commodity perhaps synonymous with Bedworth – ale. A consignment of beer has been unloaded and now heads off for the many pubs in Bedworth to slake the thirst of the mining community. The goods yard at Bedworth held thirty-eight wagons. (*Author's Collection*)

BR built 4-6-0 No.75052 passes Bedworth with a passenger train, 3 May 1963. This loco came to Nuneaton in January 1963 and was transferred away in May 1965 when the ex-LMS Black Fives arrived to take over its duties. (*R. Blencowe Collection*)

Standard Class 4 4-6-0 No. 75035 spent a short time at Nuneaton between October 1962 and May 1963 and is seen here running light. (*R. Blencowe Collection*)

Bedworth Mount Pleasant Branch

Construction commenced under the Act of 14 August 1848. The short branch was brought into use in 1851. It served a colliery at Mount Pleasant, which seems to have started operations by the 1830s and closed in the 1860s. No known track plans or details of this line have been discovered so far, although the connection with the main line is shown on the original track plan and section of the line so it was certainly built.

Left: Stanier 'Crab' 6P5F 2-6-0 No. 42971 on a southbound freight just south of Bedworth on 12 May 1964. No. 42971 was built at and entered service in and was allocated to Nuneaton between June 1962 and May 1963. It was reallocated to Crewe South in June 1963 but returned to Nuneaton the following November from where it was withdrawn in the December of 1964. It was scrapped by Cashmores of Great Bridge in March 1965. (*Mike Mensing*)

Below: 'Black Five' 4-6-0 No. 44938 hurries a passenger train through Bedworth on 3 May 1963. Built at Horwich in 1945, No. 44938 was a Rugby engine at this time. It was withdrawn from Tyseley shed in October 1967 and scrapped by Cashmores of Great Bridge in March 1968. (*Roger Carpenter Collection*)

Class 8F 2-8-0 No. 48016 passes Bedworth on 3 May 1963 with a mixed freight. No. 48016 was a long-time resident at Nuneaton shed probably the whole time from nationalisation until August 1963. It was transferred away and withdrawn from Saltley shed in November 1965, and was cut up in February 1966. (*R. Blencowe Collection*)

Ivatt 2-6-0 No. 46447 passes Bedworth on 3 May 1963 with a Coventry and Leamington train. This loco was allocated to Nuneaton in September 1961 and transferred in April 1963 to Derby. It has survived because after withdrawal in December 1966 it was sold to Woodham Brothers, whose famous Barry scrapyard saved the lives of dozens of steamers and became a Mecca for rail fans. It lingered there between June 1967 and June 1972 when it was bought for preservation and now is at the Quainton Road preservation centre. (*R. Blencowe Collection*)

Newdigate Colliery Branch

A private siding agreement was entered into with the LNWR for a connection to the Coventry–Nuneaton line on 22 July 1897. A branch railway of some 2 miles in length was built connecting to the new colliery workings, which started sinking in 1898. The branch was built by Charles Baker & Sons Ltd. The exchange sidings might predate the Newdigate Colliery agreement, as there were sidings here serving Hawkesbury Collieries Speedwell pit before Newdigate Colliery was built. The exchange reception sidings here held forty-five mineral wagons. Approximately halfway along the branch, a land sale yard and loco shed was established. A spur led off the track adjacent to the LNWR into Exhall Colliery premises. The loco shed at Smorrall Lane was replaced by a larger two-road unit at the colliery in August 1961 due to reorganisation of the surface plant at the colliery, which led to the closure of the Smorrall Lane depot and a new coal preparation plant being provided, together with a land sale depot and general relaying of the colliery sidings.

Left: Lucia was Newdigate's first loco built by Andrew Barclays in 1900. It is seen shunting at the colliery in the 1950s. (*Author's Collection*)

Below: Susan was another of Newdigate's early locos. Built in 1902, it succumbed to old age earlier than *Lucia*, being withdrawn from service in 1954 and scrapped at the colliery in June 1958. At least one of its nameplates has survived. (*Author's Collection*)

Above: Newdigate Sidings signal box in 1981. The Nuneaton and Coventry line runs from left to right of this picture with a rake of wagons standing on the exchange sidings. (*Author*)

Below left: Looking towards Smorrall Lane crossing on the Newdigate branch in July 1981. (*Author*)

Below right: Another view of the line in July 1981 showing a catch point leading to an earth bank to catch any wagons running loose from the colliery. The grade down to Smorrall Lane crossing needed this protection. (*Author*)

Newdigate Colliery

Sinking of Newdigate Colliery commenced in 1898 and coal production started in 1901. Like many collieries in the Warwickshire coalfield, a small brickyard was opened, but production did not last long, being abandoned by 1915. In 1937, Newdigate was despatching 1,500 tons of coal per day in three fifty-wagon trains hauled by one of the colliery locos. Fifty empties were worked back up the branch in return.

LOCOS AT THE COLLIERY

Name/No.	Wheel/Cylinder Arrangement	Maker	Works No./Year	Notes
Lucia	0-6-0ST IC	Andrew Barclay	869/1900	Delivered new. Scrapped on site by J. & H. B. Jackson, Coventry, February 1964.
Susan	0-6-0ST IC	Hudswell Clarke	610/1902	Delivered new. Withdrawn 1954. Scrapped on site, June 1958.
No. 3	0-6-0ST IC	Peckett	1586/1922	Delivered new. Scrapped on site by George Cohen, June 1968.
No. 4	0-6-0ST IC	Peckett	1787/1933	Delivered new. Sold for scrap, November 1971.
LMSR No. 7358	0-6-0T IC			On loan from the LMS, 25 February 1933 to 8 April 1933.
Newdigate Colliery No. 1	0-6-0ST IC	Hunslet	3841/1956	Delivered new. Sold for scrap to John Cashmore Ltd, 24 October 1968.

Coventry No. 1	0-6-0T IC	North British	24564/1939	Originated at Coventry Colliery, was refurbished at Ansley Hall NCB workshops and then sent to Newdigate Colliery, 11 October 1963. During October 1965 it went to Haunchwood Colliery but returned to Newdigate late 1965 or early 1966 before going back to Haunchwood in April 1967. It has been preserved and is now residing at the Quainton Railway Society, Quainton Road, in Buckinghamshire.
-	0-6-0ST IC	Avonside Engine	1883/1922	Ex-Arley Colliery on 27 September 1968. To Baddesley Colliery, 5 July 1969.
Joan	0-6-0ST	Avonside Engine	2048/1932	Ex-Arley Colliery on 27 September 1968. Sold for scrap by November 1971.
No. 1 NCB 9 1963	4wDH	Thomas Hill/ Sentinel rebuild	126C/1964	Ex-New Lount Colliery, 10 January 1969. To Bath Yard Locoshed, 29 April 1976. Incorporated the frame of a Simplex loco.
15/2/14 NCB 20 1967	0-6-0DH	Hunslet Engine	6692/1967	Ex-Desford Colliery, 1 May 1969. To Cadley Hill Colliery, 10 August 1981.

15/3/3	0-4-0DE	Ruston & Hornsby	420139/1958	Ex-Coventry Colliery, April 1972. To N. V. Sobermai, Maldegem, Belgium, 25 October 1980.
15/2/13 NCB 17 1966	0-6-0DH	Hunslet Engine	6288/1966	Ex-Cadley Hill Colliery, 22 April 1975, and returned then on 10 July 1981.
-	0-6-0DH	Hunslet Engine	6693/1967	Ex-BMC Longbridge, 13 May 1970, to Desford Colliery, July 1970.
-	0-4-0DH	North British	27658/1957	Ex-North British on demonstration May 1958. Returned to NB, 29 May 1958.
-	0-6-0DE	Yorkshire Engine	2717/1958	Ex-Yorkshire Engine on demonstration 3 June 1958. Returned to YE after June 1958.
-	4wDH	Rolls Royce Strachan & Henshaw		Ex-S&H on demonstration 28 May 1968. Returned to S&H, 29 May 1968.

Exhall Colliery Branch

Exhall No. 4, the 0-4-0ST built by Bagnalls of Stafford prior to being sold in 1938, stands at the colliery. (*Industrial Railway Society*)

The remains of Exhall Colliery pithead buildings as they appeared in 1948. The screens that stood in the foreground had been cleared away and their attendant railway tracks taken up. Some of the buildings by this time had been turned over to other uses. A small engineering workshop had set up in one of the old buildings, but over the years the site was cleared and Bayton Road Industrial Estate now has swallowed up most of it. The building in the distance to the right of the nearest small structure looks to be the old engine shed. The only building that appears to have survived until the present day is the base of the shaft on the right, which is now incorporated into an industrial building. (*Maurice Billington*)

Exhall Colliery

Name/No.	Wheel Cylinder Arrangement	Builder	Works No.	Disposal
Lincoln	0-6-0ST IC	Manning Wardle	204/1866	Acquired from Brassey & Ballard contractor, Bedford. Sold to Awsworth Colliery Co., Ilkeston.
Exhall	0-6-0ST IC	Manning Wardle	896/1884	Purchased new. Disposal date not known but probably before 1912 when the new Exhall arrived.
Energy (Named *Hawkesbury* until 1909)	0-6-0ST IC	Hudswell Clarke	399/1893	Purchased new. Derelict in 1937, scrapped by 1938. Due to the sharp curves and light trackwork, this loco did not find much favour and was laid aside in favour of four coupled engines.
Enterprise	0-4-0ST OC	William Bagnall	1739/1907	Purchased new. Sold to South Durham Steel & Iron Co. Ltd. Storefield Pits, Northants., 1940
Exhall No. 4	0-4-0ST OC	William Bagnall	1952/1912	Purchased new. Sold to Leicestershire Colliery & Pipe Co. Ltd, *c.* 1938.
Bessie	0-4-0ST OC	William Bagnall	2272/1925	Sold to Chislet Colliery Kent, August 1938
-	0-4-0ST OC	Peckett	1823/1933	Ex-Birmingham Tame & Rea District Drainage Board 10/1939. Via C. Jones (Engineers) Ltd (hired from Cohen, dealers and scrap merchants). Disposal to Ambrose Shardlow & Co. Ltd, Sheffield, South Yorkshire, 1944–47 period. (*See Hawkesbury Colliery details.*)

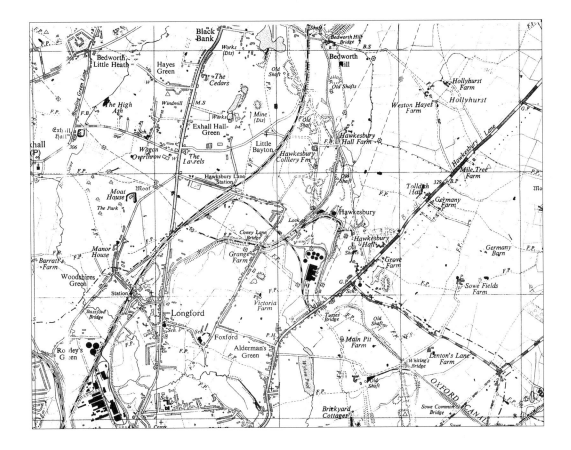

Hawkesbury Colliery

The earliest records of prospecting for coal in the Hawkesbury area date back to 1579. It was worked throughout the next 370 years, although as with other collieries in this area, it regularly suffered ingress of water and various shafts were sunk and later abandoned. To cope with water inundation, a Newcomen steam engine was installed in 1725. A Boulton & Watt engine was installed in 1776. There was also an iron furnace erected near Hawkesbury colliery in 1840. Hawkesbury was joined to Exhall Colliery in October 1939. The Hawkesbury New Winnings pit operated under new Exhall management until 1948. There might have been other locos at this site as only one is recorded and this is quite late in the life of the colliery.

Name/No.	Wheel/Cylinder Arrangement	Maker	Works No./Date	Notes
?	0-4-0ST OC	Peckett	1823/1933	See Exhall Colliery. Disposed of by 1947.

Murco Sidings

These reused the site of the former exchange sidings for Hawkesbury & Exhall Collieries Ltd and came into use by 1976. This location is still used today for petrol deliveries. Bulk trains are brought into a loop, which is the sole remaining part of the Hawkesbury marshalling yard, and then the diesel loco hooks off and the train is split. Each half is propelled back into the sidings into the two remaining tracks alongside the fuel-unloading standpipes.

Hawkesbury Lane Station

Hawkesbury Lane station opened with the line in 1850. It was a small station with low platforms and remained unchanged until the end of passenger services. In fact the building and platforms are still there today. When in 1910 the former stationmaster at Hawkesbury Lane, John Charles Blackmore, was promoted to a similar post at Hednesford station, his successor was Harry Horne. It was remarkable that at Hawkesbury Lane there were three officials named Harry Horne: the stationmaster, signalman and goods porter at this time. The signalman Harry Horne was born at Watford in 1888 and as a young man moved to Hawkesbury at the age of twenty and stayed there as signalman for forty-five years. He kept his signal box in pristine condition, decorated with flowers. It was an idyllic life. He had seven brothers who also served on the railway and Harry's son also served as a signalman on the railway at Nuneaton Trent Valley. Harry the signalman died in 1928.

Hawkesbury Lane station towards Coventry, with Hawkesbury marshalling yards beyond, 3 January 1965. (*Geoff Edmands*)

The plain waiting shelter on the Nuneaton side of Hawkesbury Lane station – a standard Crewe product. (*Maurice Billington*)

Class 8F 2-8-0 No. 48656 heads a coal train past Hawkesbury Lane heading in the Nuneaton direction. No. 48656 was a Bletchley engine for some years, was withdrawn in August 1965, and cut up between September and November that year. (*Mike Mensing*)

Hawkesbury Lane on 24 July 1948 with LMS Class 3 2-6-2T No. 143 on the 2.55 p.m. Nuneaton Trent Valley-Coventry. The Class 3s superseded the old ex-LNWR 2-4-2T in the autumn of 1941 when the increasing weight of Coventry-Nuneaton passenger trains due to wartime loadings defeated the LNWR locos on Bedworth bank and afterwards the old 2-4-2Ts were locally confined to Leicester trains and workings from Warwick Milverton shed on the Leamington Rugby and Weedon turns (*W. A. Camwell*)

Hawkesbury Marshalling Sidings

At one time, Hawkesbury Lane siding was a very important interchange point for coal traffic from collieries in the area. It handled coal traffic from as far away as Griff in addition to Charity, Exhall, Hawkesbury and Wyken as well as Coventry Colliery and for any other local traffic that needed intermediate marshalling prior to despatch . The sorting sidings could accommodate 756 wagons. A small general merchandise goods yard also opened on 21 May 1889. Wagon repairers were also accommodated here to deal with the numerous cripple wagons received weekly.

A view of Hawkesbury yard as it was in the 1980s, or what was left of it. At one time it had been used for re-marshalling coal trains heading away from the Griff and Bedworth collieries, or for assembling full trains from Exhall, Hawkesbury and Wyken collieries, so was a very busy location up until the early 1960s. A couple of sidings still survive today, one of which is used as a run round loop for petrol tank trains entering the Murco sidings. The diesel engaged on these duties has to split its train and this siding helps with that manoeuvre. The other siding is derelict. The M6 motorway bridge is in the distance. (*Author*)

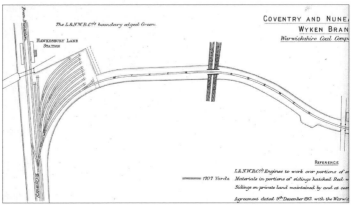

The Wyken Branch

Constructed under Acts of 14 August 1848 and brought into use in 1851, this line crossed the canal on a lightly constructed bridge. Coventry and Nuneaton loco depots retained several older and light wheel loading locomotives for working this branch. Coventry depot had several ex-MR 0-6-0s amongst its allocation. These were later replaced by LMS/BR 2-6-0s, of which Coventry had two and Nuneaton several, which interspersed passenger workings and trips over the Wyken branch. In later years, the Wyken branch was cut back to a terminus adjacent to 411 Alderman's Green Road, a length of about 1 mile.

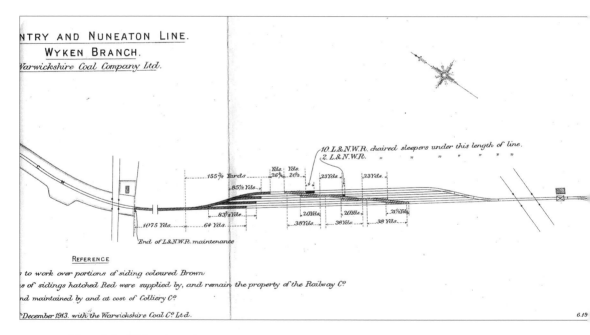

Map of the Wyken branch.

Wyken & Craven Colliery Tramway

The various collieries that eventually formed this colliery company were very old, some dating back to the sixteenth century. Prior to 1900, the collieries had a chequered history with various opening and closing dates every few years. Water was a perennial problem and Newcomen steam engines were installed in 1719, 1729, 1732 and 1734 respectively. There was also a brickworks producing red bricks, tiles and clay pipes. The colliery was later formed into a limited company.

The Wyken Coal Co. Ltd (Wyken & Craven Collieries) was a subsidiary of Markham & Co. Ltd of Chesterfield until 1916 when these two colliery workings were transferred to the Warwickshire Coal Co. Ltd.

Name/No.	Wheel/Cylinder Arrangement	Builder	Works No.	Disposal
John Liddell	0-4-0ST OC	Hawthorne Leslie	2448/1899 (New)	Sold to Macintosh Cable Co. Ltd of Derby via dealer T. W. Ward in 1928.
Emma Liddell	0-4-0ST OC	Hawthorne Leslie	2504/1901 (New)	Sold to T. W. Ward in 1928. Disposal unknown.

The locos were named after the colliery manager and his wife and were shedded at Wyken Alexandra Colliery. When this colliery closed for coal winding in January 1914, the surface installation, railway and locos were retained to handle the output of Craven Colliery, which was linked to Alexandra Colliery by means of a three quarter of a mile long rope worked tramway. Craven Colliery and the remaining Wyken shaft(s) closed in October 1927. The colliery plant was dismantled by T. W. Ward commencing in January 1928 and completed by 1930. The track was cut back to Longford power station.

The first loco at Wyken, John Liddell, was sold in 1928 to Macintosh Cable Co. Ltd and is here seen in service with that company, possibly in 1935, renamed *Macintosh*. (*M. J. Lee Collection*)

Victoria Colliery

The branch to this colliery opened on 31 May 1859. Victoria Colliery was situated on the site of Victoria Farm, Hawkesbury, and at one time six shafts were operated. Its earliest operational date is not known. The colliery closed in 1870, although the colliery connection was still *in situ* in 1874. It is known that the colliery had its own private owner wagons from photographs. There are no records of locos being used for shunting at the colliery. A new electric power station was developed on the site of Victoria colliery in 1928. This line closed in 1968.

CEGB Coventry Power Station

This power station was originally worked by Coventry Corporation and partially reused the site of the former Victoria Colliery. The station opened in 1928. It was known as Longford Generating Station and was owned by Coventry Corporation until the 1 April 1948 when it was nationalised and vested into the Central Electricity Authority.

Name/No.	Wheel/Cylinder Arrangement	Maker	Works No. Date	Notes
No. 1	0-4-0ST OC	Andrew Barclay	1942/1929	New. Scrapped 1970.
No. 2	0-4-0ST OC	Peckett	1982/1940	New. Scrapped.

The Coventry Power Station site was shunted by a Barclay 0-4-0ST No. 1. Built in 1929, it served the power station seen here feeding coal wagons through the tippler, which unloaded their contents onto a conveyor to take it to the storage area. It was one of two locos in use of the power station until being scrapped in December 1970 by Cashmore's of Great Bridge. (*M. Musson Collection*)

Longford & Exhall Station

The remains of Longford & Exhall station, which closed in 1949. Coventry gasworks can be seen the distance. The photograph was taken on 3 January 1965. (*Geoff Edmands*)

Viewed from the opposite direction, we get a view of Longford brick works on the right. This brickyard was operated by the Foleshill Brick & Tile Co. Ltd, established in 1889, although there was an earlier brickyard extant in 1850. (*Geoff Edmands*)

Coventry Gasworks

The first gasworks was operational in Coventry in 1824. A new gasworks was opened by Coventry Corporation on a site at Longford in 1909. The site is now occupied by the Ricoh stadium and retail park. The gas company was absorbed into the West Midlands Gas Board on 1 May 1949.

Name/No.	Wheel/Cylinder Arrangement	Maker	No./Date	Notes
1	0-4-0ST OC	William Bagnall	1738/1906	New. Scrapped January 1962.
2	0-4-0ST OC	William Bagnall	1959/1912	New, rebuilt by Woodwards of Marton, 1952. Scrapped October 1964.
3	0-4-0ST OC	William Bagnall	2286/1925	New. Scrapped August 1965.
4	0-4-0ST OC	William Bagnall	2674/1942	New. Scrapped 1961.
5	4WD	Ruston Hornsby	284844/1950	New. Scrapped.

Ex-LMS 2-6-2T No. 40157 heads towards Nuneaton on a local from Leamington. No. 40157 was a Nuneaton engine for some years. (*A. W. Flowers*)

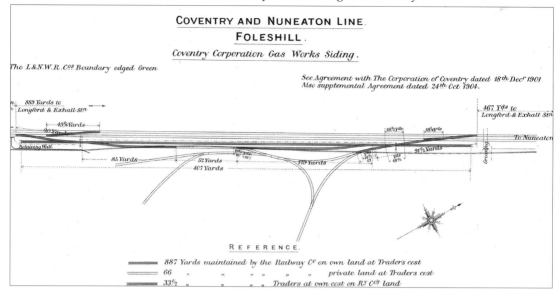

Map of Foleshill.

Coventry Gasworks siding around 1910.

Inset: On the left is the loco shed at Coventry gasworks, then newly built. The water tank alongside seems to be used for other purposes in the floors below – possibly offices or workshops. (*Author's Collection*)

One of the little four-wheeled Bagnalls at Coventry Gasworks. Coventry Corporation favoured this maker and ordered all their steam locos from them. (*Maurice Billington*)

Another Bagnall in steam. Note the very deep buffer beams. Four coupled engines were favoured because of the sharp curves that abounded in the trackwork as it threaded around the site. (*Maurice Billington*)

Coventry Colliery Sidings

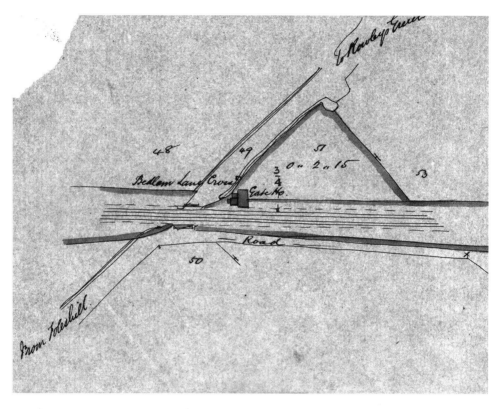

Above: Map of Coventry Colliery Sidings.

Left: Gatekeeper Gurney at Bedlam crossing gates. (*Harry Addison Collection*)

Coventry Colliery

The Warwickshire Coal Company was first registered in 1901. Sinking at Keresley, which took several years due to the ingress of water, commenced in 1911. The coal was first reached in October 1917 and full production was achieved in 1924. A branch line from the Coventry–Nuneaton line was started to be laid in 1911. The branch railway was built on former open fields formerly called 'Leightons'. Interchange sidings were put in at Three Spires Junction with a capacity for 1,600 wagons. The company owned 300 wagons and hired 700. There was a land sale at Bedlam Lane and a canal wharf at Longford on the Coventry Canal. On completion, Coventry Colliery was the largest and deepest mine in the whole of Warwickshire. By 1923, output reached 20,000 tons per week. The Warwickshire Coal Company was taken over by the Coltness Iron Co. Ltd from 1924. The arrival of Coventry Colliery brought great prosperity to the village of Keresley, which became attached to the City of Coventry through large housing developments. The Coventry Colliery closed on 16 October 1991 and the site was sold to Coal Investments Ltd on 5 April 1994. Surface railways closed in 1993. The colliery reopened in March 1994 but results were poor, leading to its final closure on 23 August 1996. The shafts were then capped. The colliery branch has been refurbished and is available for use by the Pro-Logis Distribution Park at Keresley, although at the time of writing it appears not to be in use.

Name/No.	Wheel Arrangement/ Cylinders	Maker	Works No./ Date	Notes
Renown No. 1	0-4-0ST OC	Andrew Barclay	1224/1911	Purchased new. Sold in 1933 to Netherseal Colliery Co. Ltd.
Coventry No. 1	0-6-0T IC	North British	24564/1939	Purchased new.
Coventry No. 2	0-6-0ST OC	Peckett	1662/1924	Purchased new.
Coventry No. 3	0-6-0ST OC	Peckett	1700/1925	Purchased new.
Coventry No. 4	0-6-0ST OC	Peckett	1745/1927	Purchased new.

Coventry No. 5	0-6-0T	Sharp Stewart	3449/1888	Originally built for the Barry Railway as their No. 1. It was absorbed into the GWR, becoming No. 699 before going to the Coltness Ironworks, Newmains, Lanarkshire. It came to Coventry in 1933. In 1958 it was replaced by a diesel and its final duties by March 1958 was as a pit top shunter. Scrapped on site by J. & H. B. Jackson Ltd, March 1962.
Coventry No. 6	0-4-0WT OC	Orenstein & Koppel	4734/1911?	60cm gauge. Was purchased by T. W. Ward around 1925 becoming their plant No. 35359 until 1934, when it was sold to the Warwickshire Coal Co. Ltd as Coventry Colliery No. 6 to be used on their extensive 2' 0" gauge surface system which was used for coal stacking. It did not last long and was withdrawn in 1938 after a Fowler diesel was acquired. Scrapped in June 1942 on site.
Coventry No. 7	4 wheel DM	John Fowler	21915/1938	Acquired new to work the coal stacking narrow gauge system.
William Stratford	0-6-0T OC	Andrew Barclay	1799/1923	Transferred from Baddesley Colliery, November 1958, and returned there in February 1959.
1501	0-6-0PT OC	BR WR Swindon	1949	Ex-BR via Andrew Barclay, Kilmarnock, 2 June 1962. Preserved on the Severn Valley Railway, 31 July 1970.
1502	0-6-0PT OC	BR WR Swindon	1949	Ex-BR via Andrew Barclay, Kilmarnock, August 1962. Sold for scrap to John Cashmore Ltd, Great Bridge, 23 October 1970.
1509	0-6-0PT OC	BR WR Swindon	1949	Ex-BR via Andrew Barclay, Kilmarnock, 28 March 1963. Sold to John Cashmore Ltd, Great Bridge, for scrap, 23 October 1970.

-	0-6-0 DE	Ruston Hornsby	448157	Ex-demonstrator, 3 November 1962. Returned to RH, 14 December 1962.
NCB S.M.Area No. 23	0-6-0 DH	Hunslet Engine	6689/1969	New. Scrapped on site by colliery fitters, March 1987.
NCB S M Area N.24	0-6-0 DH	Hunslet Engine	6690/1969	New. Scrapped on site by F. W. Charlton, February 1993.
-	0-4-0 DE	Ruston Hornsby	420139/1958	Ex-Ellistown Colliery, 24 September 1971. To Newdigate Colliery, April 1972.
Coventry Colliery No. 2	0-6-0 DH	Hunslet Engine	7494/1976	Ex-Daw Mill Colliery, July 1977. To Baddesley Colliery, 27 March 1979. Returned to Coventry colliery 6 February 1981. Scrapped on site by F. W. Charlton, February 1993.
Coventry Mine No. 1	0-6-0 DH	Hunslet Engine	7396/1974	Ex-Desford Colliery, September 1979. To Desford Collery, April/ May 1986.
D8740	0-6-0 DM			These 08 BR shunters were borrowed in 1986 and returned later.
D8920	0-6-0 DM			Ditto
-	6w DE	GECT	5422/1977	Ex-Littleton Colliery, 22 May 1989. To Allied Steel & Wire Ltd, Cardiff, April 1993.
-	6w DE	GECT	5478/1978	Ex-Lea Hall Colliery, 24 May 1989. To Allied Steel & Wire Ltd, 23 March 1993.
DL11	0-6-0 Dh	Yorkshire Engine	2910/1963	Ex-Bolsover Colliery, February 1990.
Charles	4 wheel DM	Ruston Hornsby	417889/1958	Ex-Trackwork, Doncaster, December 1995. Returned to Trackwork, Doncaster, January 1996.
-	4w DM	Ruston Hornsby	200793/1940	Ex-Grant Lyon Eager Ltd, Scunthorpe, 3 February 1982. Returned to Grant Lyon early 1982.

Above: The 'Star' attraction at Coventry Colliery was this six-coupled side tank, which had a long and illustrious career before it even set a wheel in motion on the Coventry Colliery layout. Built by Sharp Stewart in 1889. It displayed all the elegant lines that the builder put into their manufacturing output. There was a fine sense of balance between the chimney, dome, safety valve bonnet and cab. In short, a very fine-looking engine, and a great pity when it was scrapped because it was a historic loco as well. 'Coventry No. 5' was originally Barry Railway No. 1 and was used for many years as a front-line engine on the Barry main line railway in South Wales. The Barry Railway was absorbed into the Great Western Railway and No. 1 became their No. 699. Rebuilt at Swindon in 1922 and returned to traffic in 1923, it worked then until put on the sales list in April 1931, by which time it had amassed a mileage of 748,405. No. 699 was purchased in June 1932 by J. F. Wake of Darlington, then sold to the Coltness Iron Co. Ltd, who transferred to their subsidiary Warwickshire Coal Co. Ltd for use at Coventry Colliery, becoming 'Coventry No. 5' in 1933. The loco seems to have been newly refurbished at the colliery in this view. (*Roger Carpenter Collection*)

Opposite above: 'Coventry No. 5' again. It was scrapped in March 1962 by J. & H. B. Jackson Ltd the Coventry scrap dealer. (*M. J. Lee*)

Opposite below: 'Coventry No. 4' was a strong Peckett 0-6-0ST built in 1927. It was refurbished by Andrew Barclays, despatched there on 28 April 1963, and did not return to Keresley, going instead to Arley Colliery. It was sold to Wm Bush Ltd of Alfreton for scrap on 20 November 1969. (*K. J. Cooper*)

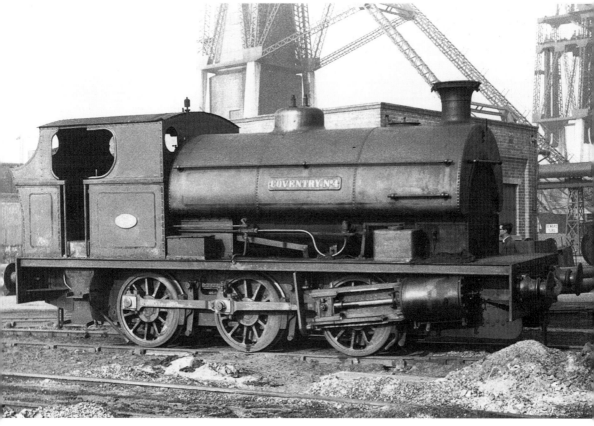

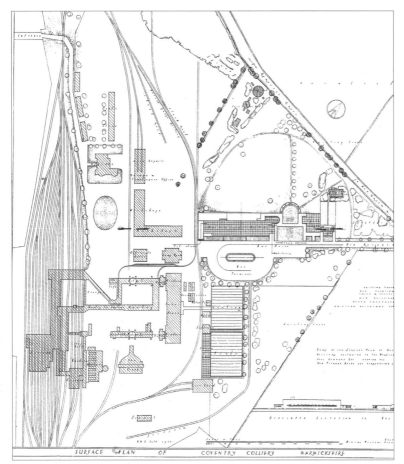

Left: The original rail layout of the colliery.

Below: Coventry Colliery obtained three of these powerful ex-Western Region of BR pannier tanks as the old steamers succumbed to old age and decrepitude. They were powerful engines, having been designed for empty passenger stock movements, which needed strong engines needing to move heavy loads over short distances. (*Industrial Railway Society*)

Prologis Park

The former colliery branch to Keresley Colliery was remodelled after closure of the colliery. After being out of use for some years, it was refurbished in 1994, but was use until February 2007, when it saw occasional use for mineral water trains to a Danone depot at Prologis Park. A standard 08 shunter has been allocated there for shunting recently.

Above left: One had to find something to do between trains on duty at Three Spires Junction, although it seems that there was not much time for leisure as the line was extremely busy, particularly during the First World War, with trains passing every few minutes. Nevertheless, Harry displays his fine euphonium, which he probably played to amuse himself in the loneliness of his cabin. It brings to mind the possibilities that being a signalman afforded, since learning to play an instrument like this between trains was ideal. Being isolated and on your own like this you did not disturb other people. Best if it was a lonely signal box on a country branch line, though, with a sparse service, as opposed to somewhere as busy as Three Spires Junction. Again, the year is 1916. (*Harry Addison*)

Above right: A general view of the Three Spires signal cabin, which was then newly opened in this sequence of 1916 views.

Three Spires Junction

Above left: The three Three Spires staff here are A. Dalby, J. Lissaman (yard inspector) and E. Randle. (*Harry Addison*)

Above right: Harry Addison sits on an empty coal wagon, which would have been worked up to one of the local collieries for filling. (*Harry Addison*)

English Electric Type 4 diesel electric D255 on the 3.45 p.m. Euston–Birmingham New Street takes a roundabout route via Three Spires Junction to Nuneaton and then via the Midland Railway route through Nuneaton via Stockingford and Whitacre Junction back to Birmingham New Street. It has been diverted due to electrification work on the main line north of Coventry, Sunday 4 September 1966.

The Coventry Loop or Avoiding Line

The Coventry Loop line extended Webster's Sidings branch, opened in 1901, a distance of 3½ miles and was opened throughout on 10 August 1914. The contractor was Holmes & King. It was sorely needed, as rail traffic congestion both on the Coventry–Nuneaton line as well as blockages in all the available sidings en route sometimes meant that it was quicker to send material by canal rather than by rail, and it is understood it once took a week to get a consignment of coal from Nuneaton to Coventry due to the pressures on the system. The Loop line increased connectivity with the businesses en route and provided a means of bypassing the operating constraints of Coventry station. There was a ruling gradient of 1 in 148 and some very heavy civil engineering works required, with a maximum height of 35 feet and depth of 31 feet. For a time, Bell Green Goods Yard was used as a dumping ground for material removed from the rebuilt Birmingham New Street station and afterwards both Bell Green and Gosford Green became shipping points for cars by rail. This only lasted a short time at Bell Green and Gosford Green later became a Freightliner depot. Closure took place on 10 November 1963 between Humber Road junction and Gosford Green, which tied in with the electrification of the London–Birmingham route; Humber Road junction to Three Spires Junction closed in 1984, and Gosford Green–Three Spires Junction closed on 26 February 1967. The Loop line has mostly disappeared under the Coventry ring road, fulfilling a function it once had as a railway, relieving the traffic around Coventry.

During the construction of the Coventry Loop line, a narrow-gauge track was laid, and one or more small contractors' locos laid on temporary track, which was moved around to various work fronts. This loco is Manning Wardle 475/1873 Exit and is seen at Courthouse Green on the site where Morris Motors was later to be erected. The loco was put up for sale on 23 July 1914 by the London & North Western Railway. It later worked on contracting work at Courtaulds main works nearby, but we have no details of disposal. (*Ray Fox Collection*)

Above: The contractors also used the usual standard gauge contractors' locos for heavier work. Here is Hunslet loco *Uxbridge*. I think this is HE761 of 1902, named because it was used as a contractor's loco on the Harrow & Uxbridge Railway. After the Coventry Loop line job, it was purchased by the Aluminium Company in 1917, where it stayed until scrapping in 1952. (*Ray Fox Collection*)

Left: Bell Green Goods Yard before the embankment on the right was removed. Evidence of the former Coventry Corporation tram track can be seen in the foreground of this photograph. This tram siding went into the goods yard from the Corporation's Stoney Stanton Road route and was used predominantly for delivery of new tram cars from the manufacturers. They could then be put on the track in the centre for transfer to the Corporation's tram depot for commissioning. The yard itself accommodated 174 wagons. (*Author's Collection*)

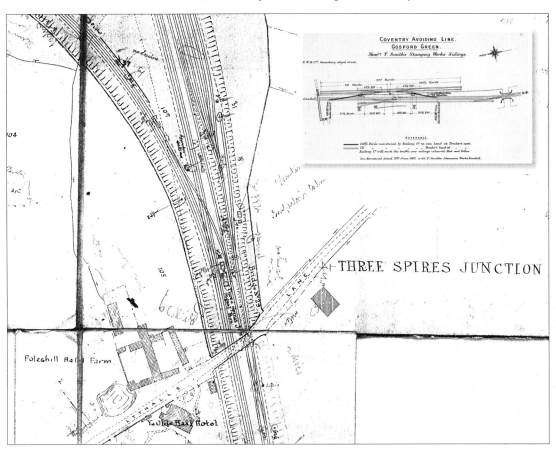

This line was authorised in 26 July 1907 Act 7, Edward 7, Chapter 87, for construction authority for the Coventry Loop line (Humber Road Junction to Three Spires Junction). Construction powers were obtained in 1910 for a line approximately 3¾ miles long. The resident engineer for the new works was Mr Hull, but when he joined the forces G. F. Trench took over as resident engineer. The contractors were Holme & King of Liverpool, but part of the way into the contract this company went into liquidation and a new contractor, John Wilson & Son Ltd of Birmingham, completed the work. Work started in August 1911. The loop was opened to goods traffic on 10 August 1914. The Pinley Junction (later Humber Road Junction, renamed on 26 July 1914) signal box was opened on 4 May 1913, and Three Spires Junction on 28 June 1914. Goods depots were established at Bell Green, which opened in 1914 and Gosford Green some months afterwards. Burlington Road and the Ordnance Sidings were opened on 14 July 1916. Burlington Road sidings were built to service a new housing scheme and the connection put in December 1915. The loop line was double track throughout with two intermediate signal boxes at Gosford Green and Bell Green. At Humber Road junction the line swept around a 25-chain curve on embankment and altogether fourteen bridges and a 6-foot subway were erected on the loop line. The yard at Gosford Green was built with four roads, a large warehouse and cattle pens. There was a brick and steel footbridge erected over the line diverting an old footpath right of way. Bell Green goods yard also had a warehouse, goods shed and signal box as well as the usual railway offices. At the same time as the loop line was built an additional loop was put in, extending three quarters of a mile to provide an additional Down road on the main Coventry–Nuneaton line. The loop line was never used for regular passenger services but there were diversions of passenger trains when maintenance work was being carried on the main lines nearby. In addition, it was traversed by various excursions including the Railway Correspondence and Travel Society's Three Spires Rail Tour, which took place on 25 November 1967.

Left: Gosford Green Goods Yard. In the 1960s, block car trains from the Rootes Group car factory in Linwood were unloaded here. Part of the site was taken over by Auto Freight Network Ltd, as their Midland car despatch railhead. When built, the yard officially held 174 wagons, the same as Bell Green. (*Author*)

Below: The Seven Branch Lines Tour on Saturday 14 April 1962 was the last passenger train over the Coventry Avoiding line. Humber Road junction was finally removed on 13 October 1963. Stop blocks were installed 33 chains from this junction. Final closure took place on 10 November 1963, Humber Road Junction – Gosford Green. A new dual carriageway relief ring road has been built over much of the former trackbed, but at this end of the line the formation survived.

Foleshill Station

Foleshill station was open for traffic seven days a week, 365 days a year, including Christmas Day. The stationmaster also looked after Coundon Road station. In November 1958, diesel railcars were introduced, which fell well short of providing sufficient seats for the large swell of passengers travelling and people opted to travel by other methods.

Above: The original Foleshill station and its curious level crossing, which seemed to be askew with regard to the road. Such primitive arrangements quickly became inadequate as Foleshill's rail and road traffic increased to a vast extent and the frequent opening and closing of level crossing gates caused a new road bridge to be built.

Right: A two-car Park Royal DMU forming the 7.10 p.m. Nuneaton–Leamington Spa has called at Foleshill station. (*Mike Mensing*)

Class 2F 0-6-0 No. 3725 has come off the road adjacent to Campton & Sons Ltd factory. The crew await their rescuers. No. 3725 was a former MR loco, which dated from 1901, so would have been well over thirty years old when this incident happened. It survived to become BR No. 58306 and was withdrawn in February 1957. (*Author's Collection*).

A view at Foleshill taken on 24 June 1961 as a northbound freight headed by ex-LNWR 0-8-0 No. 49439 (built 1901, scrapped December 1962) heads a freight towards Nuneaton. (*Mike Mensing*)

Inset: Super power for a lowly freight, but even the English Electric Type 4s came to the end of their useful lives. However, it seems premature here that one should be involved with an unfitted coal train of steel mineral wagons. The trackwork at Foleshill by this date was rationalised. D339 is the loco involved. (*Author's Collection*)

Brett's Patent Lifter Siding

Brett's Patent Lifter Co. Ltd was formed in 1898 and established a factory in Harnall Lane, Coventry. The company made drop forgings for the engineering industry. At one time it had a private siding both on the Coventry–Nuneaton line and also on the Loop line. The firm went out of business in the 1970s. The siding was disused by the 1960s.

White & Poppe Sidings

WHITE & POPPE LTD – No. 21 NATIONAL FILLING FACTORY

The Foleshill company of White & Poppe, originally founded in 1899, made engines for motor bikes and cars, and by the beginning of the First World War had premises in Holbrooks, Coventry. In June 1915 they were subcontracted by the government to fill fuses for artillery shells. This meant a very rapid erection of new buildings and the introduction of railways to the site to bring in materials and take out wagon loads of shells.

Due to wartime conditions, progress was rapid. The new railway arrangements were sanctioned by the Ministry of Munitions on 1 October 1915. The first siding was run into the factory in November 1915 and the first loco *Ciceter* arrived on site that month. Around 12,000 tons of material were handled during the first two months of operation, and the siding was intensively worked during the war years. Traffic dealt with in 1916 was 142,000 tons; in 1917, 76,000 tons and in 1918, 104,000 tons. During the war period, 50,000 loaded wagons were handled. Eventually, White & Poppes factory accommodated 6½ miles of railway track. At one stage during 1916, traffic had increased to such an extent they had to borrow a loco from the LNWR. The workforce expanded from 350 people at the start of the First World War to 12,000 during the war – mostly women. Many of these arrived by rail to add to the crush at Foleshill station. These women were dubbed 'White & Poppe Canaries' due to their being stained by the yellow explosive powder, which they handled every day. White & Poppe's ceased to trade in 1933.

Name/No.	Wheel/Cylinder Arrangement	Maker	Works No.	Notes
Ciceter	0-6-0ST IC	Manning Wardle	583/1876	Arrived during November 1915. Sold by 1920 to Adams & Benson dealers, West Bromwich, and scrapped by 1930.
Sirdar	0-6-0ST IC	Hudswell Clarke	493/1898	Arrived on 16 March 1916. Sold by 1920 later with the British Sugar Corporation, Ely factory. Sold for scrap by 1950.
Netherton	0-6-0ST IC	Manning Wardle	1603/1903	Arrived on 20 April 1916. Sold by 1920. Later hired to the Rossett Sand & Gravel Co. Ltd, which closed down and it was scrapped, June 1952.
?	?	?	?	Came from the GWR in 1916 on loan and was unsuitable, and was only used for one week.
?	?	?	?	Loco on loan from the LNWR on 21 May 1916.
Killarney	0-6-0ST IC	Hudswell Clarke	611/1902	Hired by His Majesty's Office of Works in June 1916, was unsatisfactory, and disposed of by 1920.
Bradford	0-6-0ST IC	Manning Wardle	899/1884	Arrived July 1916. Sold by 1920.
Tin Lizzie	4w PM	Manning Wardle?		Passed to the Dunlop Rim & Wheel Co. by 1922. Scrapped 1949.

All the locos above were requisitioned from private industry by the Ministry of Munitions and supplied to White & Poppe for the duration of the war.

Dunlop Rim & Wheel Co. Ltd

Name/Number	Wheel/ Cylinder Arrangement	Maker	Works No.	Notes
Tin Lizzie	4w PM	Manning Wardle?		From White & Poppe by 1922. Scrapped 1949
-	4w D (originally Petrol)	Motor Rail	2262	Ex-R. H. Neal, Park Royal, May 1928. Preserved and transferred to the Foxfield Railway, February 1968.
-	4w D	Motor Rail	5752	Ex-Associated Portland Cement, Dunstable via dealer T. W. Ward.
Dunlop No. 3	0-4-0ST OC	Andrew Barclay	1703/1920	On loan from Fort Dunlop, Birmingham, September 1961– February 1962.

In 1915, all the industrial activities in the Foleshill area caused a massive increase in the number of workers joining the passenger services here. The Dunlop Rim & Wheel arrived just after the First World War (1919) and passenger services were organised around the shift pattern of these local factories. During Dunlop's occupation of the site, the spurs installed during White & Poppe's occupation were used for inboard transportation of steel and fuel and outbound scrap. On the Coventry–Nuneaton branch, trains were often loaded to 500 passengers who were moved in seven coaches. During the inter-war years a number of company excursion trains set out from Foleshill to such places as Blackpool, Llandudno, Manchester and Alton Towers.

The Foleshill Railway

The first sod of the line to serve Messrs Webster & Co. brickworks in Stoney Stanton Road, Coventry, was cut in September 1899. The railway was to be 1 mile long and to cost between £10,000 and £12,000 to construct. The opening date was 1901 and for a few weeks the line was worked by a contractor's loco until the arrival of a new Hawthorne Leslie No. 2491 *Rosabel*. The line was extended into the works of Mulliners Ltd, a business that later became the Coventry Ordnance Works. Websters Railway was the genesis of the Foleshill Railway, which operated as a separate company from 1904 when the line to Webster's works was extended across Stoney Stanton Road through to the works of Mulliner-Wigley Ltd. This company was taken over in 1903 by Charles Cammell & Co. Ltd of Sheffield who then became Cammell Laird, shipbuilders in the same year. In 1905, the Coventry Ordnance Works became a component part of a consortium of the huge shipbuilding companies – John Brown, Cammell Laird and Fairfield. In 1905, the line was extended to Samuel Courtauld & Co. Ltd. The provision of motive power became the responsibility of the Foleshill Railway, who took over the locos. There were some extremely tight curves and grades on the Foleshill Railway. After the Coventry Ordnance Works closed in 1921, most of the traffic on the line was in connection with Courtauld's business. In 1922, Courtaulds took over the running of the railway, although there was some traffic from Jackson's scrap yard.

Name/No.	Wheel / Cylinder Arrangement	Maker	Works No.	Notes
Southam	0-4-0			

Coventry Ordnance Works

This business originated with a company called Mulliner-Wigley Ltd, which was purchased by Charles Cammell and Co. Ltd of Sheffield, a large engineering business, in 1903 – the same year they became Cammell Laird, one of the largest ship building firms in the UK. In 1905, the Coventry Ordnance Works was set up by a consortium of John Brown, Cammell Laird and Fairfields to supply gun barrels to the shipbuilding industry. Of further interest, the well-known train-manufacturing company Metro Cammell was an spinoff of this great company and this train-building firm was established in 1929. Coventry Ordnance Works also produced light weapons like machine guns, and experimented with motor cars and aircraft, but neither of these lines were pursued. The First World War was a turning point in its fortunes. From a financially struggling company prior to the war, the huge demand for its products during the war transformed the Ordnance Works' financial fortunes.

Name/ No.	Wheel & Cylinder Arrangement	Maker	Works No./ Date	Notes
Annie	0-6-0ST IC	Manning Wardle	1481/00	Ex-T. Wrigley Ltd, May 1916. Returned to same source in 1917.
Coventry (also known as *Nellie*)	0-4-0ST OC	Andrew Barclay	2053/1938	Acquired new. Sold in January 1961.
No. 10	0-4-0ST	Andrew Barclay	2039/1937	Ex-Portsmouth Dockyard. Returned there in 1946.
Darfield	0-6-0ST IC	Hunslet	162/1976	Ex-Walter Scott & Middleton, contractors.
William Tell	0-6-0ST IC	Hudswell Clarke	710/1904	Ex-Sir Robert McAlpine & Sons Ltd. To A. R. Adams (dealers), Newport, 1925.
Lady Godiva	0-4-0ST OC	Peckett	1370/1915	New. To English Electric Co. Ltd, Stafford Works
Kitchener	0-4-0ST OC	Peckett	1025/1906	New. To English Electric Co. Ltd, Stafford works temporary loan, sold for scrap at Coventry.
Peeping Tom	0-4-0CT OC	Andrew Barclay	1582/1916	New. Transferred to English Electric, Rugby works. Scrapped 1951.
Peeping Tom No. 124	4WD	Ruston Hornsby	221644/ 1943	New.

Nellie (or *Coventry*) unusually bore both names, seen here during an enthusiast's visit to Coventry Ordnance Works in the 1950s. A huddle of industrial rail enthusiasts are comparing notes. (*M. J. Lee*)

Peeping Tom was originally at the Coventry Ordnance Works but is seen here after transfer to Rugby Willens Works. The large projectile on the top is where the crane used to be attached, but had been dismantled while at the Ordnance Factory. (*Industrial Railway Society*)

Courtaulds

Name/No.	Wheel/Cylinder Arrangement	Maker	Works No./Date	Notes
Rosabel	0-4-0ST OC	Hawthorn Leslie	2491/1901	Worked at Webster Hemmings brickyard from new in 1901, then taken over by the Foleshill Railway in 1904 until 1926 (or possibly 1923) when it was transferred to Courtaulds Celanese works at Spondon Derby, where is was renamed *Henry*. Returned to Courtaulds, Coventry, on 22 March 1974 for preservation. Now in the Coventry Transport Museum.
Progress	0-4-0ST OC	Peckett	1611/1923	Acquired new, disposed of February 1952, preserved at Bugle in Cornwall.
Rocket	0-4-0ST OC	Peckett	1722/1926	To the Standard Gauge Steam Trust, Tyseley for preservation, 3 June 1974.
Rosabel	0-4-0ST	Hawthorne Leslie	3669/1927	Ex-Wolverhampton works loan August 1954–November 1954, and between January 1956 and June 1956.
-	0-4-0P	Bagnall	1442/1925	To Flint Works, 1943.
		Peckett	2085/	Preserved at Embsay on the Yorkshire Dales Railway.
Sentinel	4WTG Vertical Boiler	Sentinel	9596/1955	To Courtaulds, Great Cotes Works, Grimsby, August 1965.

Courtaulds loco *Rocket* (Peckett 1722 of 1926) in steam probably for the last time on the occasion of a 'last steaming' event held on 8 April 1972. The factory had remained steam operated until Courtaulds converted their boilers from coal to gas in 1972. The Foleshill railway closed on 29 February 1972. *Rocket* is now at Tyseley Railway Museum. (*Maurice Billington*)

Courtaulds vertical boilered Sentinel S9596/1955 was transferred to Courtaulds Great Cotes Works, Grimsby, in August 1965. (*Maurice Billington*)

Rocket outside its shed on the Foleshill Railway. (*Maurice Billington*)

Widdrington Siding or Coventry Cotton Mill Siding

A long siding to the Coventry Cotton Mill was laid in by agreement with the LNWR dated 22 April 1861. A signal box had been erected by 1870, although it almost certainly was commissioned with the new siding when that was brought into use. The mill suffered a catastrophic fire on 3 December 1891. The insurance company paid for the factory to be rebuilt, but the owners did not wish to resume business on the site and the rebuilt premises then lay empty. The Daimler Company took over the mill in 1896 and the site became known as the Motor Mill. The site covered 12 acres and was chosen by the company after having visited other potential locations around the Midlands where there were large empty factories for sale. The former cotton mill was ideal, especially with its excellent road, rail and canal connections. The Daimler site was also shared with The New Beeston Cycle & Motor Company and the Great Horseless Carriage Co. The former Cotton Mill became the first full-scale motor manufacturing plant in England. In 1897, the first car was produced and from that day forward Coventry became synonymous with car production, leading to many of the country's great car marques: Morris, Standard, Hillman, Humber, Jaguar, etc. The signal cabin protecting the junction was closed on 23 November 1914, although it may have been replaced by a ground frame as use of the siding continued.

Daimler Halt

Daimler Halt was opened on 23 November 1914. A most unusual and bold experiment took place in February 1914 with a petrol-engine railcar, which was built by the Daimler company and kept at the Radford factory, near Daimler Halt. It was a single car unit and anticipated the later railcar by thirty years. It was used for a short time on the Nuneaton, Coventry & Leamington line and also reached Rugby and Northampton on some services, but the outbreak of the First World War seemed to bring the experiment to an end. Daimler halt closed on 18 January 1964.

Two-car Metro Cammell DMU on the 1.10 p.m. Nuneaton TV–Leamington Spa passing Daimler Halt on 16 January 1965. (*Mike Mensing*)

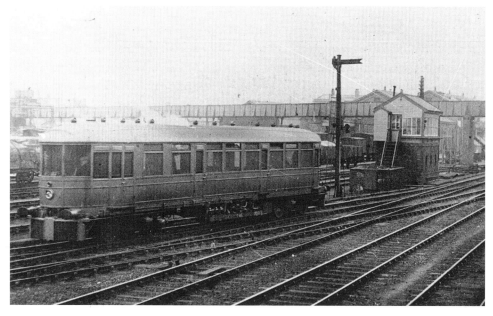

This was an experiment that was carried out on the Coventry–Nuneaton line in 1914, a petrol-electric railcar built by a joint collaboration of the Daimler Company and the BSA Company in Birmingham. It was capable of reaching 60 miles per hour and was forty years ahead of its time. It could be driven from both ends. Designed to accommodate sixty passengers sitting in comfort or 103 including standing passengers, it entered service in April 1913. It can be seen here leaving Coventry station. Like all of these early experiments with railcars, there were problems with the flexibility of using a unit with limited capacity, without the ability to attach additional vehicles and the First World War killed the experiment. Detail of its disposal is not currently known. (*Author's Collection*)

Radford Station

When the Coventry to Nuneaton line opened, a station was erected next to the Radford Road overbridge. This station does not appear to have opened or if it did it was quickly closed, by the first Ordnance Survey maps in the 1880s the building is shown in plan but not marked as an open station. It does not appear in any of the public timetables in later years. It does show up on the Coventry and Nuneaton track plan as built, clearly marked Radford station, complete with platforms as seen on page 120 in the original plan. The building lasted well over a century, still being there in the 1960s. The station house was demolished and the site cleared.

Daimler Co. Ltd

The Daimler Car Co. operated its own private siding from the Coventry line from 1896, and used a variety of locos for shunting purposes. The exact date of this siding going out of use is not recorded.

Name/No.	Wheel/Cylinder Arrangement	Maker	Works No.	Notes
St George	0-6-0ST	Manning Wardle	1003/1887	Ex-T. Oliver & Sons, contractors, Salford. Sold to Sir Robert McAlpine, contractors, 1919.
-	0-6-0T	Robert Stephenson & Co.		Details of acquisition unknown, sold by 1919.
-	0-4-0ST OC	Hawthorne Leslie	3182/1916	Purchased new. Sold to T. Walmsley, Sons & Co. Ltd, Bolton, April 1948.
-	4wD	Ruston Hornsby	235513/1945	Purchased new. Disposal not known.

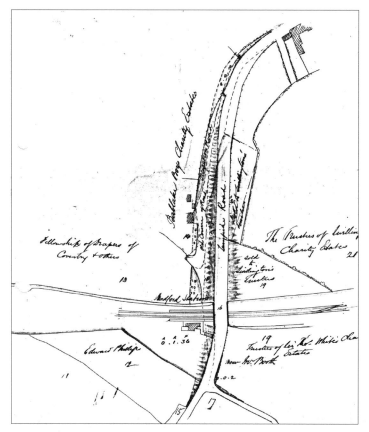

Left: Radford station.

Below: Daimler were engaged in munitions manufacture during the First World War and in this view these shells have been manufactured by Daimler and are being loaded into open wagons by the company's loco – probably the RSH given in the list below. (*Author's Collection*)

Coundon Road Station

Counden Road station was renamed Coundon Road on 1 November 1864. A notable incident at Coundon Road occurred on 6 December 1963 when Stanier 8F No. 48263 crashed through a stop block at Coundon Road station. It took ten days to recover the engine when it was hauled up and re-railed by Wellingborough and Rugby based cranes.

Right: Coundon Road station totem, 10 January 1965. (*Geoff Edmands*)

Below: Map of Coundon Road.

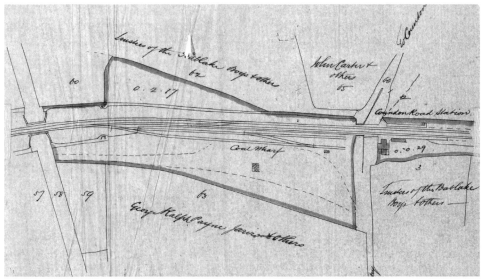

Coundon Road station looking towards Coventry on 10 January 1965; the station closed six days later. (*Geoff Edmands*)

A Class 5 4-6-0 on a Leamington-Nuneaton stopping train. (*Author's Collection*)

An undated photograph, but likely to be from before the First World War. A works photograph showing the new wagon built for the LNWR and used to convey coke between Wolverton and Coundon Road. I assume it was conveyed to Coventry Gasworks for filling. (*HMRS*)

Spon End Arches

The first stone of these arches was laid in June 1848 and the viaduct was completed in June 1849. It consisted of twenty-eight arches. The *Coventry Standard* in 1888 reported that the red sandstone arches had been unsafe for some time before the collapse of twenty-three arches of the stone-built Spon End Viaduct in the early hours of Monday 26 January 1857. The collapse shook the neighbourhood. The stone was obtained from a quarry known as Conduits Meadow Quarry at Rosehill. The first evidence of the fall of the viaduct was on the preceding Sunday night when a few stones fell out. Around one o'clock the next morning, a large part of the viaduct fell down with a thunderous noise, which woke the neighbourhood. The timing of the fall was fortuitous as in the early hours of the morning no trains were passing. Later, other parts of the bridge gradually gave way until twenty-three of the arches lay in a great pile of rubble in the road. The River Sherbourne was also blocked by the debris and the local mill was inundated. It was said that the stone used was not strong enough for the purpose of building such a tall and heavily trafficked viaduct. During the reconstruction, a horse omnibus was run from Coventry station to Coundon so that passengers could take the train from there in the Nuneaton direction. The line did not reopen until 1 October 1860 and the line was worked as a dead-end branch from the Nuneaton end while reconstruction was carried out. The collapsed arches were either rebuilt with blue bricks or replaced by an embankment. A story was told in the Coventry Standard that the contractor, on being applied to in respect of the insecurity of the arches and abutments just prior to their fall, said they would last as long as he lived, and that he died the day before the accident happened! (*Author's Collection*)

A photograph taken from a train window as it passed over Spon End arches, and looking towards the city centre sometime in the 1950s. Two of Coventry's distinctive three spires are clearly seen. (*Author's Collection*)

The complex of lines at the north end of Coventry station shows the former London & Birmingham line heading in the direction of Birmingham with the junction of the Coventry line to the right with the Coventry goods yard still *in situ*. The photograph is undated but was probably taken in the 1970s. (*Maurice Billington*)

Coventry Goods

There was a remarkable transition in the commercial life of the city in the 1860s. It all started in one small workshop where a very few hands were engaged in the manufacture of sewing machines. A business carried out by a gentleman called James Starley (1831–81) turned the skills of Coventry watchmakers and silk-ribbon weavers, who had fallen on hard times, to the manufacture of sewing machines and in 1868/69 to bicycles. The cycle trade evolved in motorcycles, cars, lorries, aircraft, etc., and components for the same were supplied to businesses all over the country, then to general engineering, iron founding, stampings, forgings, machining and all the myriad trades spun off from that first industrial innovation. It reached its zenith in the two world wars when Coventry was the military manufacturing heart of England with tens of thousands of workers engaged in the munitions industries. Much of this trade entered on to the railway system at Coventry goods depot as well as the industrial sidings referred to earlier. The LNWR (and the MR) did a huge cycle trade at the beginning of the twentieth century. Both railway companies had their own offices and goods-handling facilities at Coventry station. Cycles were bulky commodities and need a lot of packaging inside the crates to ensure the product reaches its destination safely. Therefore, the goods facilities at Coventry had to be very commodious to cope. The railway's cartage department collected the bicycles ready crated from the various factories in special double deck vans capable of holding fifty-five cycles. Freight trains were made up for destinations all over the country. It was not unusual for 900–1,000 bicycles at a time to be despatched in one train. In 1905, one cycle manufacturer turned out 10,000 machines in a month, while others were despatching 1,500 a week. There was also a vigorous export trade. All of this entered the railway system at Coventry.

Right: Brand new bicycles packed in LNWR vans, loaded in Coventry Goods Yard. (*LNWR Gazette*)

Far right: Another photograph from the *LNWR Gazette* that shows the bikes being readied for despatch with a selection of Coventry goods department staff in attendance to mark the visit of the official photographer. (*LNWR Gazette*)

Coventry Station

Coventry station was opened when the northern section of the London & Birmingham opened between Rugby and Birmingham (Curzon Street) on 9 April 1838, the original building being on the Warwick Road. Alterations and additions to the station were progressive, with new buildings being erected in 1840. A second station was built in 1860, with further additions in 1901–03. Modernisation took place on the Up side, which was completed in 1939. The war prevented work being started on the Down side and this situation lasted until the station was entirely rebuilt in the period 1958–62.

The Warwick & Leamington Union Railway was incorporated in 1842 (5 Victoria, Session 2, Chapter 81). The route was authorised on 18 June 1842 as an independent company and was sold to the London & Birmingham in 1843 as an offshoot from the London & Birmingham Railway at Coventry to Warwick (Milverton), with a capital of £130,000 and loans to the extent of £43,000. The line commenced 7 chains east of Coventry station and ran southwards, calling at Kenilworth as an intermediate station a distance of 5 miles from Coventry. Warwick (Milverton) was the original terminus. The original line was 8 miles 52 chains long. The line was opened as a single-track branch on 9 December 1844, by an Act dated 16 July 1846 (9 & 10 Victoria, Chapter 204). The London & Birmingham, Grand Junction and Manchester & Birmingham Railways were amalgamated to form the London & North Western Railway, and in an Act (9 & 10 Victoria, Chapter 248) the Coventry to Warwick line was authorised to be extended a distance of 66 chains to Leamington Spa (Avenue) station, which opened next to the Great Western station in 1852. By an Act of 1847 (10 & 11 Victoria, Chapter 278) the LNWR was authorised to make a line from Kenilworth Junction 76 chains north of Kenilworth station to Berkswell Junction on the Rugby and Birmingham main line. The design of the whole line was carried out by Mr. Robert B. Dockray (1811–71), resident engineer, to the London & Birmingham Railway.

(*Courtesy of Locomotive Magazine*)

A rare sight. No. 6004 was the very last Claughton in service, and was latterly shedded at Edge Hill, and seems to have found itself being used to position a vehicle on the end of a Rugby train on 8 August 1937. The driver, Charlie Norman, is having a good look around. This fine engine seems to be superpower on meagre shunting duties even for a Claughton towards the end of its short career. The outbreak of war lengthened the lives of the last two remaining Claughtons and No. 6004 was withdrawn in 1948. (*L. G. Copeland*)

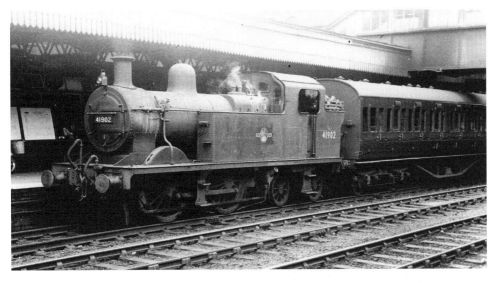

Passenger services on the Coventry branch were worked for a short time into Nuneaton with one of the LMS 0-4-4Ts. In this case, Nos 41902, 41902 and 41909 were transferred from Bletchley to Rugby district to work motor trains and this engine was allocated to Warwick Milverton shed in August 1956. No. 41909 had been transferred to Warwick shed earlier in September 1955. No. 41902 was transferred from Watford and had been sent to Warwick to replace the last of the Webb 5-foot 6-inch tanks No. 46604. In November 1958, with the end of the push/pull services on the Nuneaton, Coventry & Leamington service, the two were made redundant and returned to Rugby as stand by engines but saw little further use and both were taken out of service in 1959. For a time No. 41900 of the same class was allocated to the GWR shed at Leamington after Warwick shed closed and used on the Nuneaton parcels services.

An unusual working for coal tank No. 58897 in 1950 also featured on a Leamington–Nuneaton motor train. No. 58897 was built in 1883 and withdrawn in November 1950. (*H. F. Wheeler, Roger Carpenter Collection*)

A fine sight – Compound 4-4-0 No. 41167 heads through Coventry station probably on a Birmingham–London express in July 1955. Built in 1925, it was withdrawn in 1958. (*H. F. Wheeler*)

The ex-LMS 0-4-4Ts were built with parts that were in stock at Derby and were widely regarded as a stop-gap design, which was an economy measure at the height of the recession in 1932 when new locomotive production was curtailed. No. 41900 was shedded for a short time at Leamington Spa GWR shed after Warwick Milverton closed and used on the Nuneaton parcels service. This earned the loco a few months' reprieve as it was withdrawn in 1962, three years later than the rest of the class. (*Roger Carpenter Collection*)

A motor train departing Coventry station towards Leamington on 17 September 1952. The connection from Platform 1 to the Leamington branch was taken out in November 1974 and not replaced. (*H. F. Wheeler*)

In January 1958, work started on the entire reconstruction of Coventry station, which entailed moving 7,000 tons of earth that ended up at Bletchley, where the soil and rubble was used in the construction of a new viaduct there. During this period, use was made of the Coventry Avoiding line and the Berkswell–Kenilworth Junction line for diversions. The new station was opened in time, on 1 May 1962, for the visit of Queen Elizabeth to attend the consecration of Coventry Cathedral on 25 May 1962. (*Author's Collection*)

During the reconstruction, with access to all platforms reduced to a slippery footbridge, it was necessary to transfer parcels and mail traffic (and infirm passengers) by use of a small four-wheel diesel shunter and a single open wagon. Here is North British-built diesel shunter No. D2911 on such duties as parcels dropped from a down train at Platform 4 are chucked into the truck so they can be moved into the parcel depot for sorting. Heaven forbid that there should be any bone china, or fine glassware in those packages, or that it should rain or snow whilst all this went on. A family look on, bemused at all the frantic activity, 13 June 1961. The new electric trains started running from Birmingham to London in January 1965 with a journey time of 88 minutes. (*Michael Mensing*)

Coventry Loco Shed

LOCOMOTIVES ALLOCATED TO COVENTRY

Shed Code 8C, 9 March 1930.

Power Classification	Wheel Arrangement	No.	BR No.	Notes
LMS				
4F	0-6-0	4058	44058	Mixed Traffic wdn 1963
Ex-LNWR				
2F	0-6-0	8103		wdn 1932
2F	0-6-0	8104	58324 (did not carry number)	wdn 8/1948
2F	0-6-0	8105	58325 (did not carry number)	wdn 8/1948
2F	0-6-0	8107	58327	wdn 6/1952
2F	0-6-0	8459		wdn 4/1937
2F	0-6-0	8460	58385 (did not carry number)	wdn 9/1948
2F	0-6-0	8462		wdn 1932
2F	0-6-0	8463		wdn 3/1934
2F	0-6-0	8464	58386 (did not carry number)	wdn 10/1948
1P	2-4-2T	6689		Motor fitted 1931, wdn 11/1937
1P	2-4-2T	6690		Motor fitted 9/1932, wdn 3/1947
1P	2-4-2T	6691	46691 (did not carry number)	wdn 3/1948
7F	0-8-0	8960		wdn 12/1930
7F	0-8-0	9051	49051	wdn 2/1957
7F	0-8-0	9127	49127 (did not carry number)	wdn 3/1950
7F	0-8-0	9271	49271	wdn 11/1957
7F	0-8-0	9351	49351	wdn 11/1949

LNWR SUB-SHED OF RUGBY

1935 shed code 8C. 1935–7/1950 shed code 2F; 7/1950–11/1958 shed code 2D.

Class	Wheel Arrangement	No.	Allocation Dates	Notes
2MT	2-6-0	46420	1957	wdn 9/1966
2MT	2-6-0	46445	1951, 1954	wdn 7/1966
2MT	2-6-0	46446	1951, 1954, 1957	wdn 12/1966
3F	0-6-0T	47338	1957	wdn 1962
7F	0-8-0	8892 (48892) (number not applied)	1948	wdn 1/1949
7F	0-8-0	9135 (49135) (number not applied)	1948	wdn 11/1949
7F	0-8-0	49167	1948	wdn 12/1957
7F	0-8-0	49278	1948	wdn 10/1959
7F	0-8-0	49330	1951,1954	wdn 3/1959
7F	0-8-0	49340	1948	wdn 8/1959
7F	0-8-0	49368	1948	wdn 3/1959
7F	0-8-0	49411	1957	wdn 10/1961
7F	0-8-0	49415	1957	wdn 11/1962
7F	0-8-0	49423	1948	wdn 11/1961
7F	0-8-0	49425	1957	wdn 9/1962
7F	0-8-0	49440	1948,	wdn 3/1962
7F	0-8-0	49441	1951, 1954, 1957	wdn 10/1961
7F	0-8-0	49442	1951, 1954, 1957	wdn 11/1959
7F	0-8-0	49444	1951	wdn 10/1961
7F	0-8-0	49446	1951,1954	wdn 4/1964
2F	0-6-0	58187	1948	wdn 7/1957
2F	0-6-0	58199	1948	wdn 12/1959
2F	0-6-0	58211	1948	wdn 7/1953
2F	0-6-0	58217	1948, 1951, 1954	wdn 10/1959
2F	0-6-0	58278	1951, 1954	wdn
2F	0-6-0	58293	1948, 1951, 1954	wdn 1/1961
2F	0-6-0	58301 (did not carry number)	1948	wdn 4/1948
2F	0-6-0	58306	1951, 1954	wdn

After closure, Coventry shed was used for a short period in the early 1960s to store withdrawn steam locos laid off from Nuneaton and Rugby districts prior to scrapping.

The 'old' shed at Coventry before it was rebuilt. The photograph was probably taken in the 1930s with ex MR 0-6-0 No. 3726 parked in front of the shed, with a primitive coal stage to the left. The original two-road shed had been extended to four roads. The ex MR 0-6-0 No. 3726 was built in 1901 and allocated BR number 58307, being withdrawn in November 1950. (*H. F. Wheeller*)

Coventry loco depot plays host to ex-LNWR 4-4-0 No. 5320 the pioneer engine of the 'George the Fifth' class – named *George the Fifth*. Built in 1910 it was renumbered 25320 but never had this number applied and was withdrawn in February in 1936. It bears a No. 8 (Rugby) shed code. (*Roger Carpenter's Collection*)

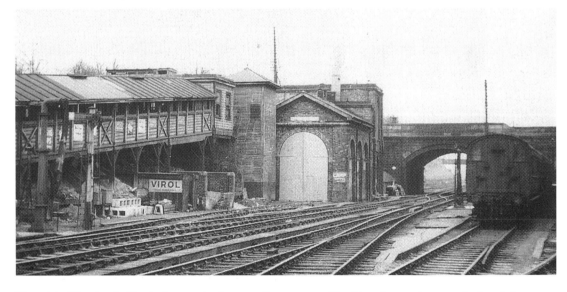

The original London & Birmingham engine house at Coventry, capable of housing one loco, survived until the 1958 rebuilding of the station. It was superseded for locomotive purposes when the new loco depot at Coventry was brought into use opened in the 1860s, and survived another ninety or more years more or less intact. (*Locomotive & General Railway Photographs*)

A general view of the south end of Coventry station, with the Leamington line off to the right, 22 April 1958. The shed site was very cramped. (*H. C. Casserley*)

A general layout view of Coventry shed on 8 November 1958. Class 3 tank No. 40135 is nearest to the camera. The 2-6-2T was a Nuneaton-based engine during this period, and was withdrawn from that shed in November 1962. No. 1 signal box is in the distance. (*H. F. Wheeler*)

Inside Coventry loco shed, 22 April 1958, with Stanier Class 3 tank 40204. This engine was a Nuneaton engine from nationalisation until withdrawn in November 1959 and Black Five 45242. The latter was a Liverpool Edge Hill engine at this time and was taken out of service in June 1967. Both locos are in steam in this view. (*H. C. Casserley*)

Coat of Arms Bridge,
Coventry

Above: The line to Kenilworth just south of Coventry passed over this stone bridge with its elaborate coat of arms attached. This is a pre-First World War view. (*Author's Collection*)

Left: A view of the single-line section between Coventry and Kenilworth on 17 August 1963, with Stanier Class 5 4-6-0 No. 44771 in charge of the 9.20 a.m. Llandudno–Leamington train. (*Mike Mensing*)

Kenilworth Junction

On 2 March 1884, the Kenilworth Junction to Berkswell line was brought into use, and the section of track from Leamington to the new line doubled. This required the former stations affected to be rebuilt. There was only one regular passenger train over this line in the 1960s: the 7.57 a.m. SO and 7.59 a.m. SX Leamington Spa Avenue to Birmingham New Street. It was extensively used during the reconstruction of Coventry station for diversionary trains. The Kenilworth Junction to Berkswell line closed to passengers on 18 January 1965 and completely on 17 January 1969.

The exchange of tokens as a DMU leaves the single-line section towards Kenilworth. The junction was 1,742 yards north of Kenilworth station. The line leading off on the extreme right leads to a long stretch, which was called 'Street's Siding'. (*Coventry Evening Telegraph*)

An ex-LNWR D (9120) passes Kenilworth Junction light engine in the late 1930s heading towards Leamington. The Berkswell branch is off to the left. No. 9120 started life as a Class B Compound in 1902, being rebuilt in the form we see here in September 1938. It was renumbered as 49120 in BR LMS stock it survived until September 1959. (*Gordon Coltas*)

On Sunday 29 April 1963, 8F 2-8-0 No. 48559 of Rugby shed has been handed the token for the single-line section and starts towards Coventry with an engineer's train. The train had been propelled off the Berkswell line. (*Mike Mensing*)

Ex LNWR 5-foot 6-inch tank 2-4-2T No. 6660 on a Leamington–Coventry motor train in the 1930s. 6660 dated back to 1893 and was scrapped in September 1947. (*Gordon Coltas*)

Ex-LNWR 0-6-0 18-inch Coal Engine No. 8450 brings a Coventry–Leamington passenger train off the Coventry section at Kenilworth Junction, probably in the 1930s. Dating from 1898, it became No. 58381 and was withdrawn in June 1952. (*Roger Carpenter Collection*)

LMS Class 4 0-6-0 No. 4360 prepares to pass Kenilworth Junction on its way towards Leamington with a coal train off the Berkswell line in the 1930s. (*Roger Carpenter Collection*)

A Type 4 diesel D255 heads the diverted 10.13 a.m. Birmingham New Street to London Euston on Sunday 6 December 1964, diverted due to engineering work on the main line. The Berkswell line diverges to the left. (*Mike Mensing*)

Class 2MT 2-6-2T No. 41228 moves off onto the single track section on a Motor Train in 1957. The signalman has retreated into his box. Old drivers have told me that a signal man here was very 'house-proud' and would not let a footplate man, if stopped here and climbing to the box to find out why he was held, enter the cabin for fear of polluting the floor of the box with coal laden boots because it would make a mess of the signalman's immaculately clean lino. This was a Warwick engine until October 1958 when it was transferred to Rugby, and it travelled widely ending up at Nine Elms on the Southern region, where it was withdrawn in July 1964. (*Gordon Coltas*)

Street's Siding

A siding was laid in before 1883, authorised 22 March 1878, which was known as 'Street's siding' or 'Mill End' siding. The user was Henry Street, and the connection served his skin works. It was controlled by a ground frame. The siding was very steeply graded down a wooded valley. Later it was also used by the Kenilworth Gas Light & Coke Co. until 1926, when that undertaking was taken over by the Coventry Corporation Gas Depot, which operated until 30 April 1949, when it was part of the West Midlands Gas Board. The siding remained listed under the WMGB auspices until 1956 at least and remained *in situ* until the 1960s. There were other users of the siding: Robbins & Powers, and later L. B. Stickley Ltd are mentioned.

Cherry Orchard Brickworks

There was a siding here operated by a ground frame, released from the signal box by Annett's Key.

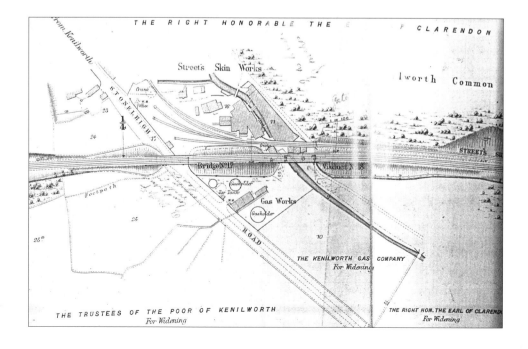

Whitemoors Brickyard

This brickyard was owned successively by Hawkes & Joberns in the 1890s, and part of site was occupied by Walter J. Lockhart from 1904. The siding opened in 1872 and was out of use by the early 1950s. The brickyard was cleared.

Above: Ex-LNWR 2-4-2T No. 6749 brings a Nuneaton–Leamington service into Kenilworth. Built in 1897, No. 6749 survived into BR days being renumbered 46749 and withdrawn February 1952. The photograph is dated 1936. Whitemoor brickyard siding is off to the right. (*Gordon Coltas*)

Right: An early view with an unidentified LNWR 0-6-0 engaged in shunting movements transferring wagons through the station. (*Author's Collection*)

Kenilworth Station

The Coventry–Milverton line opened on 9 December 1844, and a new station was erected in 1883; both stations had two platforms. The need for rebuilding came about through the construction of the line to Berkswell and the doubling of the section of track from Leamington (the track beyond Kenilworth towards Coventry remained single). There were goods yards north and south of the station. The north yard was originally a coal wharf and in 1883 it had become a general goods yard with a wooden goods shed. This goods shed survived the closure of the station and lasted until 1983. The south yard had a coal wharf and a cattle dock. The stationmaster's house also survived the demolition of the station. The domed and panelled booking hall was destroyed by fire in April 1923.

The coming of the railway stimulated the tourist trade to visit Kenilworth for its famous castle. In 1854, a party of 400 made the journey to Kenilworth by train from the Banbury Mechanics Institute. Excursions then ran for many years. Kenilworth station closed for passengers in November 1964 and for goods in January 1965 and was demolished.

An old stone-built weighbridge building from Kenilworth goods yard, dating back to the opening of the line in 1844, was taken down, packed and transported to Shackerstone on the 'Battlefield Line' in Leicestershire at the cost of Niall Bailey, the Coventry-based builders' merchant's, who took over the former station site for use as a builders merchants suppliers in the 1960s. The Battlefield line intended to re-erect it at the south end of their loco shed as a mess room for loco staff.

Kenilworth station.

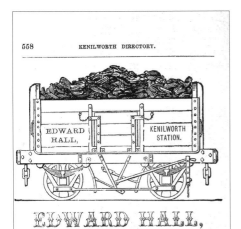

Above left: Advert for Edward Hall.

Top right: Michelin railcar No. 3 calls at Kenilworth on its way to Coventry 1937. (*Gordon Coltas*)

Above right: Kenilworth station, *c.* 1932, with an unidentified ex-LNWR 'Precursor' class 4-4-0 in charge. We get a glimpse of the busy goods yard. (*Roger Carpenter Collection*)

Below: Ex-LNWR No. 6754 on a stopping train 1938. No. 6754 was built in 1897 and scrapped in December 1947. (*Gordon Coltas*)

Left: In 1861, there was a bridge collapse at Leek Wootton with the tragic loss of lives of both of the footplate crew. The engine involved was a long-boilered McConnell o-6-o hauling a train of coal wagons including private owner wagons from Victoria Colliery near Exhall. It was mentioned during the subsequent enquiry that before the collapse had happened, local people had commented on the 'rotten' condition of this bridge, which led to its being nicknamed the Crackley Bridge. The condition of several cast-iron bridges caused some of them to be replaced by the LNWR. (*Warwickshire Libraries*)

Middle: Another view of this bridge collapse, which illustrates the entire devastation that the structure suffered. (*Warwickshire Libraries*)

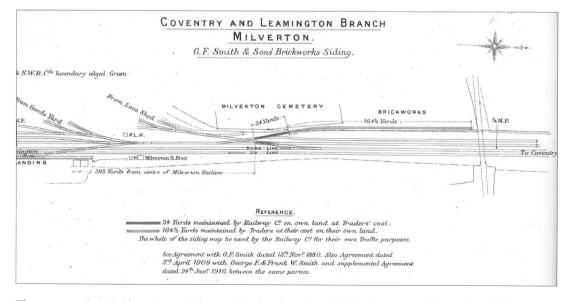

The company G. F. Smith & Sons (Brickmakers) Ltd had a private siding adjacent to Milverton loco shed at least from 1880 until the site was taken over by James Simms around 1938–40. The scrap yard continued to trade until the 1980s although the siding was probably taken out of use in the 1960s.

Warwick Milverton

Most Coventry line stations terminated at Leamington Avenue, stopping at Milverton en route. The majority of Rugby & Weedon line trains started at Warwick (Milverton) then stopped at Leamington (Spa) Avenue on their way to those destinations. Although Milverton opened as the Warwick terminus of the new line, it was rebuilt in 1883 when the line was doubled. In the nineteenth century, the name of the station changed from Warwick to Warwick (Milverton) to Leamington (Milverton) to Leamington Milverton (Warwick) to Milverton (for Warwick) then, in 1884, Warwick (Milverton), which was retained until closure.

Right: Warwick terminus.

Below: A general view of Milverton station in the 1950s.

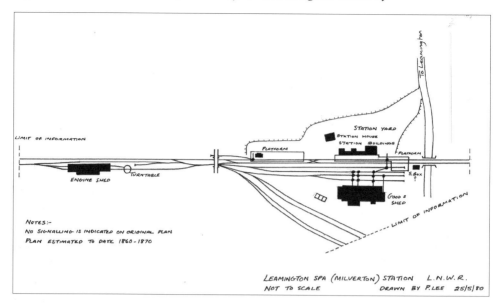

The layout of the original Milverton station, goods yard and loco shed from the original track plan and section. Note that the platforms are on the same side of the line but still could be used independently by trains going in opposite directions.

This photograph has always been attributed to have been taken at Milverton station and shows one of Mr McConnell's 'Small Bloomers'. No. 630 was built in 1854. The 'Small Bloomers' worked through services to both Birmingham and Nuneaton until the 1880s. The loco displays a destination board – Leamington– on the buffer beam. No. 630 was withdrawn in 1882. (*Author's Collection*)

Warwick Loco Shed

An order for the construction of an engine house at Warwick was made on 8 February 1844 to accommodate two engines. By 1855, it was described as the 'Leamington' shed, having room for stabling six engines. In 1880, the allocation had grown to twenty locomotives. Shortly afterwards, a new six-road shed was authorised and this was the conventional LNWR Webb standard northlight pattern. It then had a capacity of twelve locos inside the building. The shed was variously known as 'Milverton' coded 8M or Warwick coded 8W. It was a sub-shed of Rugby. Most of the shed work was providing locos for local passenger trains to Weedon, Rugby and to Nuneaton, or light freight and pick up goods. It was a very busy place in its day. In 1938 the shed was proposed to be completely modernised with a 60-foot 0-inch turntable, and a new coal and ash plant. The turntable was installed but the coal and ash plant never materialised. The outbreak of war stopped the modernisation work being carried out. By 1954 the shed allocation was down a dozen locos.

With increasing dieselisation and rationalisation of local workings, the shed closed to steam on 17 November 1958, and its remaining duties taken over by the Western Region shed at Leamington Spa. The building stood roofless and derelict for a few years afterwards and the site is now covered by housing. During its last years, Milverton was well known amongst enthusiasts as the final home of the old Webb 5-foot 6-inch 2-4-2Ts and several here lasted until the class was finally scrapped in the mid-1950s. The last No. 46654 was withdrawn in September 1954, whereas two which had been here on loan, Nos 46601 and 46666, were withdrawn in December 1953 and June 1954 respectively.

WARWICK MILVERTON SHED ALLOCATION LIST

LNWR Shed code 8W until 1935. From 1935–7/1950-2E, 7/1950–11/1958 code 2C.

Power Class	Wheel Arrangement	No.	Dates allocated	Notes
3MT	2-6-2T	40002	1951	wdn 11/1959. The Fowler 2-6-2T's took over the working of the ex LNWR 'Precursor' tanks
3MT	2-6-2T	40009	1948	wdn 5/1962
3MT	2-6-2T	40016	1951	wdn 7/1961

3MT	2-6-2T	40044	1948	wdn 11/1959
3MT	2-6-2T	40076	1951,1954,1957	wdn 10/1961
	2-6-2	40078	1951,1954, 1957	wdn 11/1962
3MT	2-6-2T	83, 40083	1945,	wdn 11/1962
3MT	2-6-2T	109, 40109	1945, 1948	wdn 7/1962
3MT	2-6-2T	135, 40135	1945, 1948	wdn from Nuneaton shed in 11/1962
3MT	2-6-2T	144, 40144	1945	wdn 12/1961
3MT	2-6-2T	40156	1954	wdn 10/1961
3MT	2-6-2T	40157	1954	wdn 11/1962
3MT	2-6-2T	40203	1948, 1957	wdn 7/1962
3MT	2-6-2T	40205	1954	wdn 11/1962
2MT	2-6-2T	41227	1948, 1951, 1954, 1957	wdn 9/1964
2MT	2-6-2T	41228	1951,1954, 1957	wdn 7/1964
2MT	2-6-2T	41239	1951	wdn 6/1964
2MT	2-6-2T	41285	1954, 1957	wdn 12/1966
4P	2-6-4T	42316	1957	wdn 1963
4P	2-6-4T	42671	1951,	wdn 1962
4P	2-6-4T	42674	1951, 1954, 1957	wdn
2F	0-6-0	3738, 58308	1945	wdn 4/1959
5MT	0-6-0	44915	1948	wdn 12/1967
5MT	4-6-0	45150	1948	wdn 3/1968
5MT	4-6-0	45191	1948	wdn 7/1967
5MT	4-6-0	45282	1948	wdn 5/1968
1P	2-4-2T	6646	1945	wdn 5/1947
1P	2-4-2T	6653	1945	wdn 5/1947
1P	2-4-2T	6669 (46669) not applied	1948	wdn 9/1949
1P	2-4-2T	6673, (46673) not applied	1945, 1948	wdn 4/1948
1P	2-4-2T	46683	1948, 1951	wdn 2/1953
1P	2-4-2T	6723	1945	wdn 5/1947
1P	2-4-2T	46749	1948, 1951	wdn 2/1952
7F	0-8-4T	47931	1948	wdn 1951
7F	0-8-4T	47932	1948	wdn 1949
8F	2-8-0	48012	1951, 1954, 1957	wdn 4/1968
8F	2-8-0	48018	1951, 1954, 1957	wdn 10/1967
7F	0-8-0	8897, (48897) not applied	1945, 1948	wdn 10/1949
7F	0-8-0	8910, (48910) not applied	1945, 1948	wdn 1/1948

7F	0-8-0	8922, (48922) not applied	1945, 1948	wdn 1/1948
7F	0-8-0	8924, (48924) not applied	1945, 1948	wdn 12/1948
7F	0-8-0	49024	1957	wdn 2/1957
7F	0-8-0	49120	1954	wdn 9/1959
7F	0-8-0	9384, (49384) not applied	1945, 1948	wdn 12/1948
7F	0-8-0	49430	1951	wdn 12/1964
2F	0-6-0	58213	1948	wdn
2F	0-6-0	58290	1951	wdn 6/1954
2F	0-6-0	58308	1948, 1951	wdn 4/1959
2F	0-6-0	28487, (58388) not applied	1948	wdn 11/1950
2F	0-6-0	28531, (58404) not applied	1948	wdn 1/1950
2F	0-6-0	28315	1945	wdn 11/1947
2F	0-6-0	28367	1945	wdn 11/1947
2F	0-6-0	28532, (58405) not applied	1945	wdn 7/1948

Warwick Milverton shed in 1929 with a nice selection of ex-LNWR ready for work: ex-LNWR 0-6-0s (18-inch goods) Nos 8455 and 8453 and an unrecognised 'D'. No. 8455 was built in 1898 and must have been withdrawn shortly after this photograph was taken as its withdrawal date was September 1929. No. 8453 built the same year lasted a bit longer until 1931. (*Gordon Coltas*)

Left: A well-filled tender obscures the identity of an ex-LNWR type between duties. (*Roger Carpenter Collection*)

Above: Ex-LNWR Precursor tank No. 6790 stands on Milverton shed probably in the 1930s. Built in 1906, it was withdrawn in February 1940. (*Stanley J. Rhodes*)

The coal stage at Milverton on 29 April 1956 with No. 73005. This engine was a long way from its home district as it was a Perth engine at this time. (*Mike Mensing*)

This photograph was taken from a passing train of Milverton shed, probably 1965, as it sped past and by this time the shed was roofless and ready for demolition. (*Author's Collection*)

An unidentified ex-LMS Class 4 0-6-0 pulls a freight towards Leamington in 1950 alongside Princes Drive. (*Gordon Coltas*)

Two ex-LNWR 0-6-0s, Nos 8450 and 8513, provide ample power for a local passenger train alongside and above Princes Drive in Leamington Spa in 1938. No. 8450 was built in 1898, renumbered 58381 and withdrawn in June 1950. No. 8513 was built in 1900 and was never renumbered by BR, with its allocated number 58397 being withdrawn in March 1950. (*Gordon Coltas*)

A Black Five ex-LMS Class 5MT 4-6-0 No. 44771 hauls the empty stock of 9.20 a.m. ex-Llandudno after it had run rounds its train at Leamington, 17 August 1963. It was a Rugby-based engine but was withdrawn from Chester shed in March 1967 and scrapped the following October. (*Mike Mensing*)

Leamington Spa Avenue Station

In 1864, exchange connections were put into the Great Western for the facilities of transferring freight over GWR metals. A new bay was added to the station Down platform in 1884 to coincide with the opening of the Berkswell line. The Rugby branch opened on 1 March 1851. Both the LMS and GWR stations were operated totally separately. In 1927 there were nineteen departures for Coventry and three direct workings to Birmingham via Kenilworth and Berkswell Junctions. Ten trains were also worked in from Rugby, four from Weedon and two from Napton & Stockton. Thirty-eight trains per day each way traversed the Leamington–Warwick (Milverton) section. By the 1950s, road competition had reduced passenger numbers and made the Rugby and Weedon services uneconomic. The line to Weedon closed on 15 September 1958. The Leamington to Rugby line closed on 15 June 1959.

A general view of Leamington Spa Avenue station in the 1950s. A porter stands in the four foot! (*Author's Collection*)

Ex-LNWR 4-4-2T Precursor Tank No. 6826 with cattle wagons in 1936. Built in 1909, it did not long survive this picture being taken, withdrawn in December 1938. (*Gordon Coltas*)

An ex-LMS Compound 4-4-0 No. 1122 prepares for a getaway with a very light train sometime in the late 1930s. Built at Horwich works in 1925, it was withdrawn in 1958. (*Gordon Coltas*)

A well turned-out Compound Class 4P 4-4-0 No. 1157 waits on a local passenger train in 1937. No. 1157 was an LMS-built compound of 1925. Built by the North British Company, it was one of the last of its class withdrawn in 1960. (*Gordon Coltas*)

A Fowler Class 3 2-6-2T No. 17 (later 40017) rests in the platform at Avenue station, probably in the 1930s. No. 40017 spent many years at northern sheds before being withdrawn in November 1959. In later years it was back in the Rugby district. (*Gordon Coltas*)

In 1938, ex-LNWR D 0-8-0 No. 8922 is shunting empty coaching stock, *c.* 1938. This engine survived nationalisation, becoming No. 48922 and was scrapped in May 1959. (*R. S. Carpenter Collection*)

Ex-MR 2F 0-6-0 No. 58290 on a Nuneaton–Leamington train in April 1951. No. 58290 was a Milverton engine at the time, built in 1897 and scrapped in June 1954. (*H. F. Wheeller*)

Ex-MR 2F 0-6-0 No. 58278 rests between duties in this tranquil summer scene. The tender looks well stocked with coal but some may have fallen off into the six foot. At any rate, the footplate crew do not seem interested. A can of tea brews by the firehole door. This loco, although in fine fettle when this photograph was taken, only survived in BR days until September 1954. No. 58278 was shedded at Coventry when the photograph was taken. (*Author's Collection*)

A nearly new motor-fitted Ivatt Class 2 2-6-2T No. 41218 in 1949. Based at Northampton shed (1951, 1963) and withdrawn from that depot in July 1965, it was scrapped in October 1965. A selection of LMS posters can be seen to the right. (*Roger Carpenter Collection*)

Another general view of the station, 1950s. (*Author's Collection*)

Class 2MT 2-6-2T No. 41235 is in charge of a push-pull working to or from Nuneaton, *c.* 1952. It was based at Nuneaton during this period and was transferred away in July 1953. No. 41235 was withdrawn in November 1962 and scrapped at Crewe Works in February 1963. (*Roger Carpenter Collection*)

Stanier Class 5MT 2-6-0 No. 2966 runs light through Leamington Spa station in 1938. No. 42966 was withdrawn in August 1964 and was for quite a few of its later years a Crewe-based engine. (*Gordon Coltas*)

Ex-LNWR 4-6-0 No. 25648 *Queen of the Belgians* passes light along the platform and is possibly running around the train on the right in 1947. Built in 1915, *Queen of the Belgians* was one of the last 'Prince of Wales' class locos to survive into nationalisation. It was allocated the No. 58000 but was withdrawn without receiving its October 1948. (*Roger Carpenter Collection*)

A two-car Birmingham Rail Carriage & Wagon Works DMU backs into the station to work the 4.15 p.m. train to Nuneaton, 24 June 1961. (*Mike Mensing*)

A three-car Metro-Cammell DMU backs out of the sidings to cross over to Avenue station after refuelling at the WR loco depot, 17 May 1962. (*Mike Mensing*)

Closure and Reopening

The Beeching Plan was published in 1963 and the Nuneaton, Coventry & Leamington passenger services were deemed uneconomic. The Nuneaton and Coventry section was scheduled to close on 16 November 1964 but was granted a short reprieve. The last train from Coventry left at 7.10 p.m. on Saturday 16 January 1965, and the official closure to passenger traffic is given as 18 January 1965. Substitute bus services were provided. Leamington Spa Avenue, Milverton and Kenilworth stations, together with all those on the Coventry section, were closed from that date. A new connection was commenced in November 1965 facilitating through running direct from the line onto the GWR at Leamington. This was brought into use on 15 May 1966, and released the trackage through the Leamington Spa Avenue station for complete closure. Work on demolishing Milverton and Kenilworth stations had started by January 1969. The Berkswell loop closed on 17 January 1969 and lifting commenced in May 1970. After singling of this line, the work of lifting was completed by July 1973. With the opening of the new Birmingham International stations, through services started running again over the Leamington–Coventry section from 12 May 1977. All coal traffic from Coventry Colliery to Didcot power station ceased over the line in 1991.

Freight facilities were removed from Bell Green Goods Depot on 5 July 1965, although this site was used as a dump for spoil from the reconstruction of Birmingham New Street station in January 1966. The last steam loco to work from Nuneaton shed was No. 75018 on the Nuneaton–Coventry parcels and 8F 48320 on the Nuneaton–Coundon Road pick up goods; after this BR Type 2 and 4 diesels took over these jobs, although they were short lived. All signalling was removed from the Coventry Loop by March 1967. Murco opened a petrol depot in on the old Exhall colliery sidings site in November 1967. Three oil refineries served this site: Thames Haven, Ellesmere Port and Lindsey. The Wyken Colliery branch was lifted during May and June 1969. A new rail terminal for car trains assembled at Gosford Green station was opened on 6 September 1968. The official opening date of the new terminal, operated by the Rootes group, was 11 February 1970. Traffic ceased on the Foleshill Railway on 29 February 1972. The Gosford Green car traffic only lasted six years until it ceased on 1 July 1976, but was temporarily saved when the depot was taken over by Freightliner, who commenced running Linwood car trains on 7 December 1977. Freightliner traffic ceased in September 1981.

Rail traffic to Newdigate Colliery closed on 26 June 1981 due to the structurally unsound condition of the road bridge carrying the main road over the line at Black Bank. The colliery did not close until February 1982. Much of the track from the Coventry Loop line was lifted by August 1982 and was sent to Northampton for reuse.

Passenger trains started to use the Leamington to Warwick line in 1977 when some Inter City trains were rerouted from Oxford towards Birmingham. This was done to allow these trains to serve Birmingham International station, which was built in 1976 to serve both the National Exhibition Centre and Birmingham Airport.

On Tuesday 10 May 1988, the first train arrived at 11.22 a.m. at the newly reconstructed Bedworth station. This was followed by a formal reopening on 16 May 1988. A full Nottingham, Leicester, Nuneaton & Coventry diesel service was introduced, although at the time of writing the service is purely a single coach Class 153 Nuneaton–Coventry service. Reopening of the through route to Leamington, with new stations at Bermuda Park, the Ricoh stadium and Kenilworth, should reinvigorate the through route, but its days of generating vast amounts of freight traffic from the industries along the route are now gone forever.